CIVIL WAR WOMEN

"Elegant or restrained, proud or self-deprecating, the voices in this collection resound." —Publishers Weekly

"Fascinating . . . an innovative look at war through the eyes of the other half of the human race." —Linda Brinson, Southern

"Valuable . . . conveys the breadth of experience of black and white, Northerner and Southerner sharing a national tragedy." —Library Journal

"The stories give us an interesting insight into the values and virtues of that time." —School Library Journal

CIVIL WAR WOMEN

AMERICAN WOMEN SHAPED BY CONFLICT IN STORIES BY ALCOTT, CHOPIN, WELTY AND OTHERS

Edited by Frank McSherry, Jr., Charles G. Waugh and Martin Greenberg

August House / *Little Rock*
PUBLISHERS

Published by August House, Inc.,
P.O. Box 3223, Little Rock, Arkansas, 72203,
501-663-7300.

Printed in the United States of America

10 9 8 7 6 5 4 3 2

LIBRARY OF CONGRESS CATALOGING-IN-PUBLICATION
DATA

Civil War women / edited by Frank McSherry, Jr., Charles G. Waugh, and
Martin Harry Greenberg.
p.   cm.
ISBN 0-87483-061-3 : $8.95
1. United States — History — Civil War, 1861-1865 — Women — Fiction.
2. United States — History — Civil War, 1861-1865 — Fiction.
3. Women — Fiction. 4. Short stories, American — Women authors.
I. McSherry, Frank D. II. Waugh, Charles. III. Greenberg, Martin Harry.
PS648.C54C54   1988
813'.01'08352042—dc19
88-6242
CIP

Cover design by Bill Jennings
Production artwork by Ira Hocut
Typography by Diversified Graphics, Little Rock, Arkansas
Design direction by Ted Parkhurst
Project direction by Hope Coulter

This book is printed on archival-quality paper which meets the guidelines for
performance and durability of the Committee on Production Guidelines for
Book Longevity of the Council on Library Resources.

AUGUST HOUSE, INC.   PUBLISHERS   LITTLE ROCK

Contents

Acknowledgments

"Hear the Nightingale Sing" by Caroline Gordon, from *The Collected Stories of Caroline Gordon*, copyright © 1961, 1963, 1977, 1981 by Caroline Gordon. Reprinted by permission of Farrar, Straus, and Giroux, Inc.

"Turkey Hunt" by Alberta Pierson Hannum, copyright © 1937. Reprinted here by permission of Curtis Brown, Ltd.

"The Burning" by Eudora Welty, copyright © 1951, 1979 by Eudora Welty. Reprinted from her volume *The Bride of the Innisfallen* by permission of Harcourt Brace Jovanovich, Inc.

Introduction

WAR, LIKE NO other subject, has been considered the province of men. When cultures collide, it is the experience of males, from Roman footsoldiers to twentieth-century generals, that is usually chronicled by historians, playwrights, and fiction writers, epic poets and film producers.

But there has always been another side to war—the woman's view. Someone packs the knapsacks of those warriors and bids them goodbye. Someone turns back to mundane labors, to the day-to-day responsibilities of a life that has suddenly, drastically changed. Someone runs the small farms and businesses that feed the hyperactive economies of wartime. Someone rears the next generation, and answers its questions about the killing of this one.

For American women, the Civil War was a major watershed. It would have dominated the lives and minds of any people, of course, in terms of human and material damage alone: 618,000 American men were killed in the war, and many thousands of others suffered wounds or prison deprivations; national economies were crippled. And men and women shared a psychological toll as well. For Southerners there was the shock of seeing familiar domestic scenery turned into battlegrounds and wasteland. For both sides, the challenge to an ideal of national unity was painful.

But for women in particular, this war happened at a time in their collective self-understanding that made its impact great. In the mid-nineteenth century, American women had begun to develop a political voice. They had started the temperance and abolitionist movements that swept the nation, fueling the moralistic fervor that contributed to the outbreak of war. Opposition to these activities, stirred up by those who considered it beyond the proper sphere of women's concerns, had—ironically—turned the reformers' focus more upon themselves and

7

their own condition. In 1848 the Seneca Falls Convention at Seneca Falls, New York, had marked the formal, concerted beginning of the women's movement. This new assertiveness was reflected in literature too. Inspired by their sisters in Europe, American women were writing and publishing in numbers—sometimes hesitantly, with a cast of sentiment, piety, or self-deprecation, but often boldly and with resonance. By the 1860s, in the course of their shouldering the roles that men naturally assumed during peacetime, women began to gain a new understanding of themselves. This self-image appears, in a fascinating array of forms, in the stories of *Civil War Women*.

Some of these stories were written at the time of the Civil War and some many years later. Some center on Unionists and some on Confederates. They vary from the taut action of Caroline Gordon's "Hear the Nightingale Sing" to the languor of Grace King's "Bayou l'Ombre." Some, like Alberta Pierson Hannum's "Turkey Hunt," indict the violence of war; in others, like Elsie Singmaster's "The Battleground," a heroine embittered by her losses sadly decides that war may nonetheless be a means to justice. "Bayou l'Ombre" and Kate Chopin's "The Locket" explore how girls learn to romanticize war. But what stands out in all these works is the heroines' vigor. Jumping on horses, jumping off horses, parceling out provisions, managing old people, managing children, dressing wounds, cooking, interminably sewing...and we think the "superwoman" high-performance standards are a phenomenon of our own day! It is a wonder these heroines have energy left to comment on their circumstances.

But they do. These stories, collected, have a larger theme that links the individual narratives—the celebration of *activeness*. Wartime, with all its deprivations and peril, gives these women a real cause into which they can pour their energies. The tasks might be as routine as nursing and sewing, or as thrilling as hiding mules in the cellar, galloping through the mountains to relay messages, or freeing prisoners under the enemy's very eyes. Wherever the deeds fall on the spectrum of realism to romanticism, what is novel to their doers is the sense of making a difference—of having some part to play, however small, in the public world that was largely off-limits to them during peacetime. These heroines learn that an active role is crucial to their full self-realization—that exertion and growth are intertwined.

The heroine in Rose Terry Cooke's story is a rather frivolous, sheltered girl who, through the suffering imposed on her by war, becomes worthy of the label she is given in the story's title: "A Woman," with all the implicit dignity of that term—committed, responsible, a source of strength to others. The same strength lives in the abolitionist nurse of Louisa May Alcott's "The Brothers," who is energetic, steady, and astute. Perhaps several of these characters, taken as a group, are moving toward the exuberant act and statement of the 70-year-old woman in Elizabeth Stuart Phelps Ward's "Comrades." That character's name, "Patience," rather exasperates her; she—like others of her day, who were discarding ideals of sweet passivity in favor of stronger models—prefers her nickname, "Peter," which more aptly means "rock." Many years after the war, Peter falls into step with her veteran husband at the annual Memorial Day parade. "'I've *earned the right to*,'" she tells him with the intensity of a person who has reflected on and accepted certain, but not all, limitations.

So far, of course, this discussion has neglected to mention American blacks. For black women, as for black men, the Civil War could not have the same overtones it did for whites. In the first place, it was the delayed result of a practice so obviously evil that it should never have been started, much less continued to this point—causing what Alcott called "the twilight [that] a great sin has brought to overshadow the whole land." Also, the slavery binding most blacks' hands kept them from being much more than pawns in a white man's power struggle. That conflict was the necessary prelude to emancipation and to many, many later battles for full enfranchisement; but, not surprisingly, the Civil War itself has not inspired much fiction by black writers, despite the flowering of Afro-American literature in the twentieth century (and the dominance of that field, in the 1970s and '80s, by women). What has been published is mainly in the form of novels, not short stories. So for the black perspective in *Civil War Women* we are left with white writers' projections—and they are telling.

Reform-minded women had been comparing their lot to the slaves' since the 1820s. Alcott's Nurse Dane dramatizes their insights in her involvement with the contraband, Robert. In her first encounter with Robert, a few neat images condense what could be whole volumes of observations about the sociology of oppression and class interaction—her noticing his austere beauty and dignity, disfigured by his wound; and both characters' vacillation, hers between the roles of sympathetic peer and curt mistress, and his between pride and servility. Later Nurse Dane ponders the rectitude of her urging Robert to a moral course of action, when he has been the victim of so much evil:

> . . .He had no religion, for he was no saintly "Uncle Tom," and Slavery's black shadow seemed to darken all the world to him and shut out God. . .What did he know of justice, or the mercy that should temper that stern virtue, when every law, human and divine, had been broken on his hearthstone? Should I have tried to touch him by appeals to filial duty, to brotherly love? How had his appeals been answered?

It is Alcott, of all the writers represented here, who ennobles the 54th regiment of the Union Army—black soldiers fighting for a republic that did not even regard them as citizens.

Far removed from Alcott's abolitionist views is the racial conscious-ness revealed in Grace King's "Bayou l'Ombre." In depicting planta-tion slaves, King portrays them either patronizingly, stressing their closeness to and dependency on their owners, or as primitive savages. Washing clothes, the slave women are described as showing

> disregard of concealment, license of pose, freedom of limb, hi-larity, conviviality, audacities of heart and tongue, joyous in-dulgence in freak and impulse, banishment of thought, a return, indeed, for one brief moment to the wild, sweet ways of nature, to the festal days of ancestral golden age (a short retrogression for them). . . .

Even the slaves' joy over a report of emancipation meets with King's scorn; she seems to think them ill-mannered for showing their enthusiasm in front of their mistresses.

But it is Delilah, in Eudora Welty's "The Burning," who provides the last, most spellbinding image here of a wartime heroine, black or white. For Delilah is a survivor. She has been a slave in a weirder world than Caliban's—a spinsters' mansion that seems built of potent illusions, including the lie that denies Delilah's motherhood. Beyond her captivity in that house, beyond rape, beyond losing her baby son, Delilah moves on—"dances," Welty says, and we see her as in an eerie ballet. We see her at her mistresses' hanging-suicide, a human stepstool who is kicked away so that one will die, but rolls away of her own volition so the second will die too. We see her looking for herself—where? In a "dim mirror" found in the ashes, an ornate looking-glass supported by gold-filigreed figurines of straining black men. She knows it is not enough. As all survivors must do, Delilah leaves the site of her degradation, and leaves behind her those women who have been both oppressors and victims. But she scavenges the best of them: their treasures and their shoes. Carrying them, and carrying the ashes of her child, she strides into the river, not to drown herself in it—she is no suicide, not she!—but to cross it.

Hope Norman Coulter

The Brothers

Louisa May Alcott

DOCTOR FRANCK CAME in as I sat sewing up the rents in an old shirt, that Tom might go tidily to his grave. New shirts were needed for the living, and there was no wife or mother to "dress him handsome when he went to meet the Lord," as one woman said, describing the fine funeral she had pinched herself to give her son.

"Miss Dane, I'm in a quandary," began the Doctor, with that expression of countenance which says as plainly as words, "I want to ask a favor, but I wish you'd save me the trouble."

"Can I help you out of it?"

"Faith! I don't like to propose it, but you certainly can, if you please."

"Then give it a name, I beg."

"You see a Reb has just been brought in crazy with typhoid; a bad case in every way; a drunken, rascally little captain somebody took the trouble to capture, but whom nobody wants to take the trouble to cure. The wards are full, the ladies worked to death, and willing to be for our own boys, but rather slow to risk their lives for a Reb. Now you've had the fever, you like queer patients, your mate will see to your ward for a while, and I will find you a good attendant. The fellow won't last long, I fancy; but he can't die without some sort of care, you know. I've put him in the fourth story of the west wing, away from the rest. It is airy, quiet, and comfortable there. I'm on that ward, and will do my best for you in every way. Now, then, will you go?"

"Of course I will, out of perversity, if not common charity; for some of these people think that because I'm an abolitionist I am also a heathen, and I should rather like to show them, that, though I cannot quite love my enemies, I am willing to take care of them."

"Very good; I thought you'd go; and speaking of abolition reminds me that you can have a contraband for servant, if you like. It is that fine mulatto fellow who was found burying his Rebel master after the fight, and, being badly cut over the head, our boys brought him along. Will you have him?"

"By all means,—for I'll stand to my guns on that point, as on the other; these black boys are far more faithful and handy than some of the white scamps given me to serve, instead of being served by. But is this man well enough?"

"Yes, for that sort of work, and I think you'll like him. He must have been a handsome fellow before he got his face slashed; not much darker than myself; his master's son, I dare say, and the white blood makes him rather high and haughty about some things. He was in a bad way when he came in, but vowed he'd die in the street rather than turn in with the black fellows below; so I put him up in the west wing, to be out of the way, and he's seen to the captain all the morning. When can you go up?"

"As soon as Tom is laid out, Skinner moved, Haywood washed, Marble dressed, Charley rubbed, Downs taken up, Upham laid down, and the whole forty fed."

We both laughed, though the Doctor was on his way to the dead-house and I held a shroud on my lap. But in a hospital one learns that cheerfulness is one's salvation; for, in an atmosphere of suffering and death, heaviness of heart would soon paralyze usefulness of hand, if the blessed gift of smiles had been denied us.

In an hour I took possession of my new charge, finding a dissipated-looking boy of nineteen or twenty raving in the solitary little room, with no one near him but the contraband in the room adjoining. Feeling decidedly more interest in the black man than in the white, yet remembering the Doctor's hint of his being "high and haughty," I glanced furtively at him as I scattered chloride of lime about the room to purify the air, and settled matters to suit myself. I had seen many contrabands, but never one so attractive as this. All colored men are called "boys," even if their heads are white; this boy was five-and-twenty at least, strong-limbed and manly, and had the look of one who never had been cowed by abuse or worn with oppressive labor. He sat on his bed doing nothing; no book, no pipe, no pen or paper anywhere appeared, yet anything less indolent or listless than his attitude and expression I never saw. Erect he sat, with a hand on either knee, and eyes fixed on the bare wall opposite, so rapt in some absorbing thought as to be unconscious of my presence, though the door stood wide open and my movements were by no means noiseless. His face was half averted, but I instantly approved the Doctor's taste, for the profile which I saw possessed all the attributes of comeliness belonging to his mixed race. He was more quadroon than mulatto, with Saxon features, Spanish complexion darkened by exposure, color in lips and cheek, waving hair, and an eye full of the passionate melancholy which in such men always seems to utter a mute protest against the broken law that doomed them at their birth. What could he be thinking of? The sick boy cursed and raved, I rustled to and fro, steps passed the door, bells rang, and the steady rumble of army-wagons came up from the street, still he never stirred. I had seen colored people in what they call "the black sulks," when, for days, they neither smiled nor spoke, and scarcely ate. But this was something more than that; for the man was not dully brooding over some small grievance; he seemed to see an all-absorbing fact or fancy recorded on the wall, which was a blank to me. I wondered if it were some deep wrong or sorrow, kept alive by memory and impotent regret; if he mourned for the dead master to whom he had been faithful to the end; or if the liberty now his were robbed of half its sweetness by the knowledge that some one near and dear to him still languished in the hell from which he had escaped. My heart quite warmed to him at that idea; I wanted to know and comfort him; and, following the impulse of the moment, I went in and touched him on the shoulder.

In an instant the man vanished and the slave appeared. Freedom was too new a boon to have wrought its blessed changes yet, and as he started up, with his hand at his temple and an obsequious "Yes, Ma'am," any romance that had gathered round him fled away, leaving the saddest of all sad facts in living guise before me. Not only did the manhood seem to die out of him, but the comeliness that first attracted me; for, as he turned, I saw the ghastly wound that had laid open cheek and forehead. Being partly healed, it was no longer bandaged, but held together with strips of that transparent plaster which I never see without a shiver and swift recollections of the scenes with which it is associated in my mind. Part of his black hair had been shorn away, and one eye was nearly closed; pain so distorted, and the cruel sabre-cut so marred that portion of his face, that, when I saw it, I felt as if a fine medal had been suddenly reversed, showing me a far more striking type of human suffering and wrong than Michel Angelo's bronze prisoner. By one of those inexplicable processes that often teach us how little we understand ourselves, my purpose was suddenly changed, and though I went in to offer comfort as a friend, I merely gave an order as a mistress.

"Will you open these windows? this man needs more air."

He obeyed at once, and, as he slowly urged up the unruly sash, the handsome profile was again turned toward me, and again I was possessed by my first impression so strongly that I involuntarily said,—

"Thank you, Sir."

Perhaps it was fancy, but I thought that in the look of mingled surprise and something like reproach which he gave me there was also a trace of grateful pleasure. But he said, in that tone of spiritless humility these poor souls learn so soon,—

"I a'n't a white man, Ma'am, I'm a contraband."

"Yes, I know it; but a contraband is a free man, and I heartily congratulate you."

He liked that; his face shone, he squared his shoulders, lifted his head, and looked me full in the eye with a brisk—

"Thank ye, Ma'am; anything more to do fer yer?"

"Doctor Franck thought you would help me with this man, as there are many patients and few nurses or attendants. Have you had the fever?"

"No, Ma'am."

"They should have thought of that when they put him here; wounds and fevers should not be together. I'll try to get you moved."

He laughed a sudden laugh,—if he had been a white man, I should have called it scornful; as he was a few shades darker than myself, I suppose it must be considered an insolent, or at least an unmannerly one.

"It don't matter, Ma'am. I'd rather be up here with the fever than down with those niggers; and there a'n't no other place fer me."

Poor fellow! that was true. No ward in all the hospital would take him in to lie side by side with the most miserable white wreck there. Like the bat in Aesop's fable, he belonged to neither race; and the pride of one, the helplessness of the other, kept him hovering alone in the twilight a great sin has brought to overshadow the whole land.

"You shall stay, then; for I would far rather have you than my lazy Jack. But are you well and strong enough?"

"I guess I'll do, Ma'am."

He spoke with a passive sort of acquiescence,—as if it did not much matter, if he were not able, and no one would particularly rejoice, if he were.

"Yes, I think you will. By what name shall I call you?"

"Bob, Ma'am."

Every woman has her pet whim; one of mine was to teach the men self-respect by treating them respectfully. Tom, Dick, and Harry would pass, when lads rejoiced in those familiar abbreviations; but to address men often old enough to be my father in that style did not suit my old-fashioned ideas of propriety. This "Bob" would never do; I should have found it as easy to call the chaplain "Gus" as my tragical-looking contraband by a title so strongly associated with the tail of a kite.

"What is your other name?" I asked. "I like to call my attendants by their last names rather than by their first."

"I've got no other, Ma'am; we have our master's names, or do without. Mine's dead, and I won't have anything of his about me."

"Well, I'll call you Robert, then, and you may fill this pitcher for me, if you will be so kind."

He went; but, through all the tame obedience years of servitude had taught him, I could see that the proud spirit his father gave him was not yet subdued, for the look and gesture with which he repudiated his master's name were a more effective declaration of independence than any Fourth-of-July orator could have prepared.

We spent a curious week together. Robert seldom left his room, except upon my errands; and I was a prisoner all day, often all night, by the bedside of the Rebel. The fever burned itself rapidly away, for there seemed little vitality to feed it in the feeble frame of this old young man, whose life had been none of the most righteous, judging from the revelations made by his unconscious lips; since more than once Robert authoritatively silenced him, when my gentler hushings were of no avail, and blasphemous wanderings or ribald campsongs made my cheeks burn and Robert's face assume an aspect of disgust. The captain was a gentleman in the world's eye, but the contraband was the gentleman in mine;—I was a fanatic, and that accounts for such depravity of taste, I hope. I never asked Robert of himself, feeling that somewhere there was a spot still too sore to bear the lightest touch; but, from his language, manner, and intelligence, I inferred that his color had procured for him the few advantages within the reach of a quick-witted, kindly treated slave. Silent, grave, and thoughtful, but most serviceable, was my contraband; glad of the books I brought him, faithful in the performance of the duties I assigned to him, grateful for the friendliness I could not but feel and show toward him. Often I longed to ask what purpose was so visibly altering his aspect with such daily deepening gloom. But I never dared, and no one else had either time or desire to pry into the past of this specimen of one branch of the chivalrous "F.F.Vs."

On the seventh night, Dr. Franck suggested that it would be well for some one, besides the general watchman of the ward, to be with the captain, as it might be his last. Although the greater part of the two preceding nights had been spent there, of course I offered to remain,—for there is a strange fascination in these scenes, which renders one careless of fatigues and unconscious of fear until the crisis is passed.

"Give him water as long as he can drink, and if he drops into a natural sleep, it may save him. I'll look in at midnight, when some change will probably take place. Nothing but sleep or a miracle will keep him now. Good night."

Away went the Doctor; and, devouring a whole mouthful of gapes, I lowered the lamp, wet the captain's head, and sat down on a hard stool to begin my watch. The captain lay with his hot, haggard face turned toward me, filling the air with his poisonous breath, and feebly muttering, with lips and tongue so parched that the sanest speech would have been difficult to understand. Robert was stretched on his bed in the inner room, the door of which stood ajar, that a fresh draught from his open window might carry the fever-fumes away through mine. I could just see a long, dark figure, with the lighter outline of a face, and, having little else to do just then, I fell to thinking of this curious contraband, who evidently prized his freedom highly, yet seemed in no haste to enjoy it.

Doctor Franck had offered to send him on to safer quarters, but he had said, "No, thank yer, Sir, not yet," and then had gone away to fall into one of those black moods of his, which began to disturb me, because I had no power to lighten them. As I sat listening to the clocks from the steeples all about us, I amused myself with planning Robert's future, as I often did my own, and had dealt out to him a generous hand of trumps wherewith to play this game of life which hitherto had gone so cruelly against him, when a harsh, choked voice called,—

"Lucy!"

It was the captain, and some new terror seemed to have gifted him with momentary strength.

"Yes, here's Lucy," I answered, hoping that by following the fancy I might quiet him—for his face was damp with the clammy moisture, and his frame shaken with the nervous tremor that so often precedes death. His dull eye fixed upon me, dilating with a bewildered look of incredulity and wrath, till he broke out fiercely,—

"That's a lie! she's dead,—and so's Bob, damn him!"

Finding speech a failure, I began to sing the quiet tune that had often soothed delirium like this; but hardly had the line,

"See gentle patience smile on pain,"

passed my lips, when he clutched me by the wrist, whispering like one in mortal fear,—

"Hush! she used to sing that way to Bob, but she never would to me. I swore I'd whip the Devil out of her, and I did; but you know before she cut her throat she said she'd haunt me, and there she is!"

He pointed behind me with an aspect of such pale dismay, that I involuntarily glanced over my shoulder and started as if I had seen a veritable ghost; for, peering from the gloom of that inner room, I saw a shadowy face, with dark hair all about it, and a glimpse of scarlet at the throat. An instant showed me that it was only Robert leaning from his bed's-foot, wrapped in a gray army-blanket, with his red shirt just visible above it, and his long hair disordered by sleep. But what a strange expression was on his face! The unmarred side was toward me, fixed and motionless as when I first observed it,—less absorbed now, but more intent. His eye glittered, his lips were apart like one who listened with every sense, and his whole aspect reminded me of a hound to which some wind had brought the scene of unsuspected prey.

"Do you know him, Robert? Does he mean you?"

"Lord, no, Ma'am; they all own half a dozen Bobs: but hearin' my name woke me; that's all."

He spoke quite naturally, and lay down again, while I returned to my charge, thinking that this paroxysm was probably his last. But by another hour I perceived a hopeful change, for the tremor had subsided, the cold dew was gone, his breathing was more regular, and Sleep, the healer, had descended to save or take him gently away. Doctor Franck looked in at midnight, bade me keep all cool and quiet, and not fail to administer a certain draught as soon as the captain woke. Very much relieved I laid my head on my arms, uncomfortably folded on the little table, and fancied I was about to perform one of the feats which practice renders possible,—"sleeping with one eye open," as we say; a half-and-half doze, for all senses sleep but that of hearing; the faintest murmur, sigh, or motion will break it, and give one back one's wits much brightened by the brief permission to "stand at ease." On this night, the experiment was a failure, for previous vigils, confinement, and much care had rendered naps a dangerous indulgence. Having roused half a dozen times in an hour to find all quiet, I dropped my heavy head on my arms, and, drowsily resolving to look up again in fifteen minutes, fell fast asleep.

The striking of a deep-voiced clock woke me with a start. "That is one," thought I, but, to my dismay, two more strokes followed; and in remorseful haste I sprang up to see what harm my long oblivion had done. A strong hand put me back into my seat, and held me there. It was Robert. The instant my eye met his my heart began to beat, and all along my nerves tingled that electric flash which foretells a danger that we cannot see. He was very pale, his mouth grim, and both eyes full of sombre fire,—for even the wounded one as open now, all the more sinister for the deep scar above and below. But his touch was steady, his voice quiet, as he said,—

"Sit still, Ma'am; I won't hurt yer, nor even scare yer, if I can help it, but yer waked too soon."

"Let me go, Robert,—the captain is stirring,—I must give him something."

"No, Ma'am, yer can't stir an inch. Look here!"

Holding me with one hand, with the other he took up the glass in which I had left the draught, and showed me it was empty.

"Has he taken it?" I asked, more and more bewildered.

"I flung it out o' winder, Ma'am; he'll have to do without."

"But why, Robert? why did you do it?"

"Because I hate him!"

Impossible to doubt the truth of that; his whole face showed it, as he spoke through his set teeth, and launched a fiery glance at the unconscious captain. I could only hold my breath and stare blankly at him, wondering what mad act was coming next. I suppose I shook and turned white, as women have a foolish habit of doing when sudden danger daunts them; for Robert released my arm, sat down upon the bedside just in front of me, and said, with the ominous quietude that made me cold to see and hear,—

"Don't yer be frightened, Ma'am; don't try to run away, fer the door's locked an' the key in my pocket; don't yer cry out, fer yer'd have to scream a long while, with my hand on yer mouth, before yer was heard. Be still, an' I'll tell yer what I'm goin' to do."

"Lord help us! he has taken the fever in some sudden, violent way, and is out of his head. I must humor him till some one comes"; in pursuance of which swift determination, I tried to say, quite composedly,—

"I will be still and hear you; but open the window. Why did you shut it?"

"I'm sorry I can't do it, Ma'am; but yer'd jump out, or call, if I did, an' I'm not ready yet. I shut it to make yer sleep, an' heat would do it quicker'n anything else I could do."

The captain moved, and feebly muttered, "Water!" Instinctively I rose to give it to him, but the heavy hand came down upon my shoulder, and in the same decided tone Robert said,—

"The water went with the physic; let him call."

"Do let me go to him! he'll die without care!"

"I mean he shall;—don't yer interfere, if yer please, Ma'am."

In spite of his quiet tone and respectful manner, I saw murder in his eyes, and turned faint with fear; yet the fear excited me, and, hardly knowing what I did, I seized the hands that had seized me, crying,—

"No, no, you shall not kill him! it is base to hurt a helpless man. Why do you hate him? He is not your master?"

"He's my brother."

I felt that answer from head to foot, and seemed to fathom what was coming, with a prescience vague, but unmistakable. One appeal was left to me, and I made it.

"Robert, tell me what it means? Do not commit a crime and make me accessory to it. There is a better way of righting wrong than by violence;—let me help you find it."

My voice trembled as I spoke, and I heard the frightened flutter of my heart; so did he, and if any little act of mine had ever won affection or respect from him, the memory of it served me then. He looked down, and seemed to put some question to himself; whatever it was, the answer was in my favor, for when his eyes rose again, they were gloomy, but not desperate.

"I *will* tell you, Ma'am; but mind, this makes no difference; the boy is mine. I'll give the Lord a chance to take him fust; if He don't, I shall."

"Oh, no! remember, he is your brother."

An unwise speech; I felt it as it passed my lips, for a black frown gathered on Robert's face, and his strong hands closed with an ugly sort of grip. But he did not touch the poor soul gasping there behind him, and seemed content to let the slow suffocation of that stifling room end his frail life.

"I'm not like to forget that, Ma'am, when I've been thinkin' of it all this week. I knew him when they fetched him in, an' would 'a' done it long 'fore this, but I wanted to ask where Lucy was; he knows,—he told tonight,—an' now he's done for."

"Who is Lucy?" I asked hurriedly, intent on keeping his mind busy with any thought but murder.

With one of the swift transitions of a mixed temperament like this, at my question Robert's deep eyes filled, the clenched hands were spread before his face, and all I heard were the broken words,—

"My wife,—he took her"—

In that instant every thought of fear was swallowed up in burning indignation for the wrong, and a perfect passion of pity for the desperate man so tempted to avenge an injury for which there seemed no redress but this. He was no longer slave or contraband, no drop of black blood marred him in my sight, but an infinite compassion yearned to save, to help, to comfort him. Words seemed so powerless I offered none, only put my hand on his poor head, wounded, homeless, bowed down with grief for which I had no cure, and softly smoothed the long neglected hair, pitifully wondering the while where was the wife who must have loved this tender-hearted man so well.

The captain moaned again, and faintly whispered, "Air!" but I never stirred. God forgive me! just then I hated him as only a woman thinking of a sister woman's wrong could hate. Robert looked up; his eyes were dry again, his mouth grim. I saw that, said, "Tell me more," and he did,—for sympathy is a gift the poorest may give, the proudest stoop to receive.

"Yer see, Ma'am, his father,—I might say ours, if I warn't ashamed of both of 'em,—his father died two years ago, an' left us all to Marster Ned,—that's him here, eighteen then. He always hated me, I looked so like old Marster: he don't,—only the light skin an' hair. Old Marster was kind to all of us, me 'specially, an' bought Lucy off the next plantation down there in South Car'lina, when he found I liked her. I married her, all I could, ma'am; it warn't much, but we was true to one another till Marster Ned come home a year after an' made hell fer both of us. He sent my old mother to be used up in his rice-swamp in Georgy; he found me with my pretty Lucy, an' though young Miss cried, an' I prayed to him on my knees, an' Lucy run away, he wouldn't have no mercy; he brought her back, an'—took her, Ma'am."

"Oh! what did you do?" I cried, hot with helpless pain and passion.

How the man's outraged heart sent the blood flaming up into his face and deepened the tones of his impetuous voice, as he stretched his arm across the bed, saying, with a terribly expressive gesture,—

"I half murdered him, an' to-night I'll finish."

"Yes, yes,—but go on now; what came next?"

He gave me a look that showed no white man could have felt a deeper degradation in remembering and confessing these last acts of brotherly oppression.

"They whipped me till I couldn't stand, an' then they sold me further South. Yer thought I was a white man once;—look here!"

With a sudden wrench he tore the shirt from neck to waist, and on his strong brown shoulders showed me furrows deeply ploughed, wounds which, though healed, were ghastlier to me than any in that house. I could not speak to him, and, with the pathetic dignity a great grief lends the humblest sufferer, he ended his brief tragedy by simply saying,—

"That's all, Ma'am. I've never seen her since, an' now I never shall in this world,—maybe not in t'other."

"But, Robert, why think her dead? The captain was wandering

when he said those sad things; perhaps he will retract them when he is sane. Don't despair; don't give up yet."

"No, Ma'am, I guess he's right; she was too proud to bear that long. It's like her to kill herself. I told her to, if there was no other way; an' she always minded me, Lucy did. My poor girl! Oh, it warn't right! No, by God, it warn't!"

As the memory of this bitter wrong, this double bereavement, burned in his sore heart, the devil that lurks in every strong man's blood leaped up; he put his hand upon his brother's throat, and, watching the white face before him, muttered low between his teeth,—

"I'm lettin' him go too easy; there's no pain in this; we a'n't even yet. I wish he knew me. Marster Ned! it's Bob; where's Lucy?"

From the captain's lips there came a long faint sigh, and nothing but a flutter of the eyelids showed that he still lived. A strange stillness filled the room as the elder brother held the younger's life suspended in his hand, while wavering between a dim hope and a deadly hate. In the whirl of thoughts that went on in my brain, only one was clear enough to act upon. I must prevent murder, if I could,—but how? What could I do up there alone, locked in with a dying man and a lunatic?—for any mind yielded utterly to any unrighteous impulse is mad while the impulse rules it. Strength I had not, nor much courage, neither time nor wit for stratagem, and chance only could bring me help before it was too late. But one weapon I possessed,—a tongue,—often a woman's best defence; and sympathy, stronger than fear, gave me power to use it. What I said Heaven only knows, but surely Heaven helped me; words burned on my lips, tears streamed from my eyes, and some good angel prompted me to use the one name that had power to arrest my hearer's hand and touch his heart. For at that moment I heartily believed that Lucy lived, and this earnest faith roused in him a like belief.

He listened with the lowering look of one in whom brute instinct was sovereign for the time,—a look that makes the noblest countenance base. He was but a man,—a poor, untaught, outcast, outraged man. Life had few joys for him; the world offered him no honors, no success, no home, no love. What future would this crime mar? and why should he deny himself that sweet, yet bitter morsel called revenge? How many white men, with all New England's freedom, culture, Christianity, would not have felt as he felt then? Should I have reproached him for a human anguish, a human longing for redress, all now left him from the ruin of his few poor hopes? Who had taught him that self-control, self-sacrifice, are attributes that make men masters of the earth and lift them nearer heaven? Should I have urged the beauty of forgiveness, the duty of devout submission? He had no religion, for he was no saintly "Uncle Tom," and Slavery's black shadow seemed to darken all the world to him and shut out God. Should I have warned him of penalties, of judgments, and the potency of law? What did he know of justice, or the mercy that should temper that stern virtue, when every law, human and divine, had been broken on the hearthstone? Should I have tried to touch him by appeals to filial duty, to brotherly love? How had his appeals been answered? What memories had father and brother stored up in his heart to plead for either now? No,—all these influences, these associations, would have proved worse than useless, had I been calm enough to try them. I was not; but instinct, subtler than reason, showed me the one safe clue by which to lead this troubled soul from the labyrinth in which it groped and nearly fell. When I paused, breathless, Robert turned to me, asking, as if human assurances could strengthen his faith in Divine Omnipotence,—

"Do you believe, if I let Marster Ned live, the Lord will give me back my Lucy?"

"As surely as there is a Lord, you will find her here or in the beautiful hereafter, where there is no black or white, no master and no slave."

He took his hand from his brother's throat, lifted his eyes from my face to the wintry sky beyond, as if searching for that blessed country, happier even than the happy North. Alas, it was the darkest hour before dawn!—there was no star above, no light below but the pale glimmer of the lamp that showed the brother who had made him desolate. Like a blind man who believes there is a sun, yet cannot see it, he shook his head, let his arms drop nervelessly upon his knees, and sat there dumbly asking that question which many a soul whose faith is firmer fixed than his has asked in hours less dark than this,—"Where is God?" I saw the tide had turned, and strenuously tried to keep this rudderless life-boat from slipping back into the whirlpool wherein it had been so nearly lost.

"I have listened to you, Robert; now hear me, and heed what I say, because my heart is full of pity for you, full of hope for your future, and a desire to help you now. I want you to go away from here, from the temptation of this place, and the sad thoughts that haunt it. You have conquered yourself once, and I honor you for it, because, the harder the battle, the more glorious the victory; but it is safer to put a greater distance between you and this man. I will write you letters, give you money, and send you to good old Massachusetts to begin your new life a freeman,—yes, and a happy man; for when the captain is himself again, I will learn where Lucy is, and move heaven and earth to find and give her back to you. Will you do this, Robert?"

Slowly, very slowly, the answer came; for the purpose of a week, perhaps a year, was hard to relinquish in an hour.

"Yes, Ma'am, I will."

"Good! Now you are the man I thought you, and I'll work for you with all my heart. You need sleep, my poor fellow; go, and try to forget. The captain is still alive, and as yet you are spared that sin. No, don't look there; I'll care for him. Come, Robert, for Lucy's sake."

Thank Heaven for the immortality of love! for when all other means of salvation failed, a spark of this vital fire softened the man's iron will until a woman's hand could bend it. He let me take from him the key, let me draw him gently away and lead him to the solitude which now was the most healing balm I could bestow. Once in his little room, he fell down on his bed and lay there as if spent with the sharpest conflict of his life. I slipped the bolt across his door, and unlocked my own, flung up the window, steadied myself with a breath of air, then rushed to Doctor Franck. He came; and till dawn we worked together, saving one brother's life, and taking earnest thought how best to secure the other's liberty. When the sun came up as blithely as if it shone only upon happy homes, the Doctor went to Robert. For an hour I heard the murmur of their voices; once I caught the sound of heavy sobs, and for a time a reverent hush, as if in the silence that good man were ministering to soul as well as sense. When he departed he took Robert with him, pausing to tell me he should get him off as soon as possible, but not before we met again.

Nothing more was seen of them all day; another surgeon came to see the captain, and another attendant came to fill the empty place. I tried to rest, but could not, with the thought of poor Lucy tugging at my heart, and was soon back at my post again anxiously hoping that my contraband had not been too hastily spirited away. Just as night fell there came a tap, and, opening, I saw Robert literally "clothed and in his right mind." The Doctor had replaced the ragged suit with tidy garments, and no trace of that tempestuous night remained but deeper lines upon the forehead and the docile look of a repentant child. He did not cross the threshold, did not offer me his hand,—only took off his cap, saying, with a traitorous falter in his voice,—

"God bless you, Ma'am! I'm goin'."

I put out both my hands, and held his fast.

"Good bye, Robert! Keep up good heart, and when I come home to Massachusetts we'll meet in a happier place than this. Are you quite ready, quite comfortable for your journey?"

"Yes, Ma'am, yes; the Doctor's fixed everything; I'm goin' with a friend of his; my papers are all right, an' I'm as happy as I can be till I find"—

He stopped there; then went on, with a glance into the room,—

"I'm glad I didn't do it, an' I thank yer, Ma'am, fer hinderin' me,—thank yer hearty; but I'm afraid I hate him jest the same."

Of course he did; and so did I; for these faulty hearts of ours cannot turn perfect in a night, but need frost and fire, wind and rain, to ripen and make them ready for the great harvest-home. Wishing to divert his mind, I put my poor mite into his hand, and, remembering the magic of a certain little book, I gave him mine, on whose dark cover whitely shone the Virgin Mother and the Child, the grand history of whose life the book contained. The money went into Robert's pocket with a grateful murmur, the book into his bosom with a long look and a tremulous—

"I never saw *my* baby, Ma'am."

I broke down then; and though my eyes were too dim to see, I felt the touch of lips upon my hands, heard the sound of departing feet, and knew my contraband was gone.

When one feels an intense dislike, the less one says about the subject of it the better; therefore I shall merely record that the captain lived,—in time was exchanged; and that, whoever the other party was, I am convinced the Government got the best of the bargain. But long before this occurred, I had fulfilled my promise to Robert; for as soon as my patient recovered strength of memory enough to make his answer trustworthy, I asked, without any circumlocution—

"Captain Fairfax, where is Lucy?"

And too feeble to be angry, surprised, or insincere, he straightway answered,—

"Dead, Miss Dane."

"And she killed herself, when you sold Bob?"

"How the Devil did you know that?" he muttered, with an expression half-remorseful, half-amazed; but I was satisfied and said no more.

Of course, this went to Robert, waiting far away there in a lonely home,—waiting, working, hoping for his Lucy. It almost broke my heart to do it; but delay was weak, deceit was wicked; so I sent the heavy tidings, and very soon the answer came—only three lines; but I felt that the sustaining power of the man's life was gone.

"I thought I'd never see her any more; I'm glad to know she's out of trouble. I thank yer, Ma'am; an' if they let us, I'll fight fer yer till I'm killed, which I hope will be 'fore long."

Six months later he had his wish, and kept his word.

Every one knows the story of the attack on Fort Wagner; but we should not tire yet of recalling how our Fifty-Fourth, spent with three sleepless nights, a day's fast, and a march under the July sun, stormed the fort as night fell, facing death in many shapes, following their brave leaders through a fiery rain of shot and shell, fighting valiantly for "God and Governor Andrew,"—how the regiment that went into action seven hundred strong came out having had nearly half its number captured, killed, or wounded, leaving their young commander to be buried, like a chief of earlier times, with his bodyguards around him, faithful to the death. Surely, the insult turns to honor, and the wide grave needs no monument but the heroism that consecrates it in our sight; surely, the hearts that held him nearest see through their tears a noble victory in the seeming sad defeat; and surely, God's benediction was bestowed, when this loyal soul answered, as Death called the roll, "Lord, here am I, with the brothers Thou has given me!"

The future must show how well that fight was fought; for though Fort Wagner still defies us, public prejudice is down; and through the cannon-smoke of that black night the manhood of the colored race shines before many eyes that would not see, rings in many ears that would not hear, wins many hearts that would not hitherto believe.

When the news came that we were needed, there was none so glad as I to leave teaching contrabands, the new work I had taken up, and go to nurse "our boys," as my dusky flock so proudly called the wounded of the Fifty-Fourth. Feeling more satisfaction, as I assumed my big apron and turned up my cuffs, than if dressing for the President's levee, I fell to work on board the hospital-ship in Hilton-Head harbor. The scene was most familiar, and yet strange; for only dark faces looked up at me from the pallets so thickly laid along the floor, and I missed the sharp accent of my Yankee boys in the slower, softer voices calling cheerily to one another, or answering my questions with a stout, "We'll never give it up, Ma'am, till the last Reb's dead," or, "If our people's free, we can afford to die."

Passing from bed to bed, intent on making one pair of hands do the work of three, at least, I gradually washed, fed, and bandaged my way down the long line of sable heroes, and coming to the very last, found that he was my contraband. So old, so worn, so deathly weak and wan, I never should have known him but for the deep scar on his cheek. That side lay uppermost, and caught my eye at once; but even then I doubted, such an awful change had come upon him, when, turning to the ticket just above his head, I saw the name, "Robert Dane." That both assured and touched me, for, remembering that he had no name, I knew that he had taken mine. I longed for him to speak to me, to tell how he had fared since I lost sight of him, and let me perform some little service for him in return for many he had done for me; but he seemed asleep; and as I stood reliving that strange night again, a bright lad, who lay next him softly waving an old fan across both beds, looked up and said,—

"I guess you know him, Ma'am?"

"You are right. Do you?"

"As much as any one was able to, Ma'am."

"Why do you say 'was,' as if the man were dead and gone?"

"I s'pose because I know he'll have to go. He's got a bad jab in the breast, an' is bleedin' inside, the Doctor says. He don't suffer any, only gets weaker 'n' weaker every minute. I've been fannin' him this long while, an' he's talked a little; but he don't know me now, so he's most gone, I guess."

There was so much sorrow and affection in the boy's face, that I remembered something, and asked, with redoubled interest,—

"Are you the one that brought him off? I was told about a boy who nearly lost his life in saving that of his mate."

I dare say the young fellow blushed, as any modest lad might have done; I could not see it, but I heard the chuckle of satisfaction that escaped him, as he glanced from his shattered arm and bandaged side to the pale figure opposite.

"Lord, Ma'am, that's nothin'; we boys always stan' by one another, an' I warn't goin' to leave him to be tormented any more by them cussed Rebs. He's been a slave once, though he don't look half so much like it as me, an' I was born in Boston."

He did not; for the speaker was as black as the ace of spades,—being a sturdy specimen, the knave of clubs would perhaps be a fitter representative,—but the dark freeman looked at the white slave with the pitiful, yet puzzled expression I have so often seen on the faces of our wisest men, when this tangled question of Slavery presents itself, asking to be cut or patiently undone.

"Tell me what you know of this man; for, even if he were awake, he is too weak to talk."

"I never saw him till I joined the regiment, an' no one 'peared to have got much out of him. He was a shut-up sort of feller, an' didn't seem to care for anything but gettin' at the Rebs. Some say he was the fust man of us that enlisted; I know he fretted till we were off, an' when we pitched into old Wagner, he fought like the Devil."

"Were you with him when he was wounded? How was it?"

"Yes, Ma'am. There was somethin' queer about it; for he 'peared to know the chap that killed him, an' the chap knew him. I don't dare to ask, but I rather guess one owned the other some time,—for, when they clinched, the chap sung out, 'Bob!' an' Dane, 'Marster Ned!'—then they went at it."

I sat down suddenly, for the old anger and compassion struggled in my heart, and I both longed and feared to hear what was to follow.

"You see, when the Colonel—Lord keep an' send him back to us!—it a'n't certain yet, you know, Ma'am, though it's two days ago we lost him—well, when the Colonel shouted, 'Rush on, boys, rush on!' Dane tore away as if he was goin' to take the fort alone; I was next him, an' kept close as we went through the ditch an' up the wall. Hi! warn't that a rusher!" and the boy flung up his well arm with a whoop, as if the mere memory of that stirring moment came over him in a gust of irrepressible excitement.

"Were you afraid?" I said,—asking the question women often put, and receiving the answer they seldom fail to get.

"No, Ma'am!"—emphasis on the "Ma'am,"—"I never thought of anything but the damn' Rebs, that scalp, slash, an' cut our ears off, when they git us. I was bound to let daylight into one of 'em at least, an' I did. Hope he liked it!"

"It is evident that you did, and I don't blame you in the least. Now go on about Robert, for I should be at work."

"He was one of the fust up; I was just behind, an' though the whole thing happened in a minute, I remember how it was, for all I was yellin' and knockin' round like mad. Just where we were, some sort of an officer was wavin' his sword an' cheerin' on his men; Dane saw him by a big flash that come by; he flung away his gun, give a leap, an' went at that feller as if he was Jeff, Beauregard, an' Lee, all in one. I scrabbled after as quick as I could, but was only up in time to see him git the sword straight through him an' drop into the ditch. You needn't ask what I did next, Ma'am, for I don't quite know myself; all I'm clear about is, that I managed somehow to pitch that Reb into the fort as dead as Moses, git hold of Dane, an' bring him off. Poor old feller! we said we went in to live or die; he said he went in to die, an' he's done it."

I had been intently watching the excited speaker; but as he regretfully added those last words I turned again, and Robert's eyes met mine,—those melancholy eyes, so full of an intelligence that proved he had heard, remembered, and reflected with that preternatural power which often outlives all other faculties. He knew me, yet gave no greeting; was glad to see a woman's face, yet had to smile wherewith to welcome it; felt that he was dying, yet uttered no farewell. He was too far across the river to return or linger now; departing thought, strength, breath, were spent in one grateful look, one murmur of submission to the last pang he could ever feel. His lips moved, and, bending to them, a whisper chilled my cheek, as it shaped the broken words,—

"I would have done it,—but it's better so,—I'm satisfied."

Ah! well he might be,—for, as he turned his face from the shadow of the life that was, the sunshine of the life to be touched it with a beautiful content, and in the drawing of a breath my contraband found wife and home, eternal liberty and God.

Hear the Nightingale Sing

Caroline Gordon

IT WAS SO dark in the ravine that at first she could not see the horses. Then her eyes grew accustomed to the gloom. She caught a gleam of white through the branches. She worked her way through the thicket and came upon Bess and Old Gray tethered to the ring that had been fixed in the trunk of a big pine. But the mule was not there.

She looked at the broken tether. "Where's Lightning?" she asked.

The horses pressed up to her, nudging at the sack that was slung over her shoulders. She took hold of their halters and led them down the hill to the branch and up the stream to a place where the hazel bushes grew higher than her head. She let them drink their fill, then left them tethered to a little cottonwood, while she went on up the hill to look for the mule.

The woods were thin between here and the pike. She moved slowly, keeping a tree always between her and the road. At the top of the hill she climbed up on a stump to look down on the pike. There was a cloud of dust off in the direction of Gordonsville but she could not see any soldiers moving along the road. She could remember times—in the first year of the war, just after all the boys had gone away—when she used to walk in the late afternoons up to the top of this hill in the hope that somebody might be passing. There had hardly ever been anybody then. Now there was almost always something moving along the road—great, lumbering army wagons, regiments of infantry marching, squads of cavalry sweeping by in clouds of dust.

There was a rustling in the bushes along the fence. There the mule stood, looking at her. He ducked his head when he saw that she was looking at him, and moved off quickly. She got down off the stump, clumsily, in her homemade shoes, and went toward him, holding out an ear of corn. "Cu-up! Cu-up!" she called in a whisper. He wheeled; his little hooves clattered against the rails. She turned and walked the other way, holding the nubbin of corn behind her back. When she felt him take hold of it she whirled and grasped his foretop. The nubbin had fallen to the ground. She stooped and retrieved it and held it before him on her open palm. "Lightning!" she said, *"Lightning!"* and slipped her arms down about his neck and closed her eyes and laid her cheek against his side.

A long time ago—winter before last—she used to go down to the stable lot early after breakfast on cold mornings and, finding him standing in his corner, his breath steaming in the frosty air, she would cry out to Uncle Joe that her little mule was freezing and put her arms about him and bury her face in his shaggy hair. Uncle Joe would laugh, saying that that mule had enough hair to keep both of them warm. "Ain't no 'count, nohow."

Once Tom Ladd had come up behind them without their hearing him. "I don't believe I'd have given you that mule if I'd known how you were going to raise him," he said. "You can't get him back now," she had told him. "I'm raising him to be the no 'countest mule in the country."

He laughed. They walked in silence over the lightly frozen ground up to the house. He had what her father called "the gift of silence." But sometimes, sitting in company, you would look up and find him watching you and it would seem that he had just said something or was about to say something. But what it was she never knew. And it might be that he never had any particularity for her. It might be that he noticed her more than the other girls only because she had the mule for a pet. He liked all animals.

She, too, had always been overfond of animals. When she was a little girl and Uncle Joe would bring a team in to plow the garden in the spring, she would look at the mules standing with their heads hung, their great, dark eyes fixing nothing, and she would think how, like Negroes, they were born into the world for nothing but labor, and her heart would seem to break in her bosom and she would run barefoot down the rows and when Uncle Joe cracked his whip she would clutch his elbow, shrieking, "You, Uncle Joe. Don't you hit that mule!" until the old man would leave his team standing and, going to the window where her mother sat, sewing, would ask her to please make Miss Barbara come in the house.

When she became a young lady it had tickled her fancy to have a mule for a pet. Lightning, nosing unreproved at the kitchen door or walking across the flower beds, seemed, somehow, to make up for the pangs she had suffered as a child. But even then, in those far-off days, when her father was still alive and the servants were all still on the place and you had only to call from the upper gallery to have somebody come and lead him back to the pasture when he trespassed—even then in those days that were so hard to remember now, he had been a trouble and a care.

He was old Lightfoot's colt. Lightfoot had gone blind in her last days. Tom Ladd had turned her over to Jake Robinson to take care of. Jake had taken good care of her but he could not resist the temptation to get one more colt out of her. Tom had some business with her father and had been spending the night at their house. A Negro boy brought word from Jake that Lightfoot had foaled in the night. They were at breakfast. Her mother had just asked her to go to the kitchen to get some hot bread. Tom Ladd said, "Miss Barbara, how'd you like to have one of Lightfoot's colts?" She was so taken aback that she did not answer. She came back with the biscuits and sat down and would have let what he had said pass unnoticed. But he looked at her as she came in and he spoke again. "It'll be her last colt."

Tom Ladd came to their house two or three times a week. A bed was kept ready for him in the office whenever he cared to spend the night. But he had never danced with her or with her sister and if he sat on the porch with them in the evenings it was to talk with her father about the crops or the stock. Tom Ladd loved horses better than people, her mother said, and he loved liquor better than he loved horses. Her father said that was because he was a bachelor, living alone in that big house, but her mother said it was in the blood: all the Ladds drank themselves to death.

She had felt her color rising, knowing that her mother's eyes were upon her. But it was no crime to love horses, and as for liquor, she had seen her father sprawling on the cellar steps, a jug in his hand. She said, "I'll have to see the colt first, Mr. Ladd."

Everybody laughed and the moment passed. After breakfast they drove over to Robinson's to see the new colt. Jake was sitting on the front steps, mending some harness. He did not quit his work, saying only, "I'll be out there in a minute, Mister Tom."

They walked out into the pasture. The mare stood at the far end, beside a willow sink. They could see, under her belly, the long, thin legs and little, wobbly feet. "Sorrel," Tom Ladd said, "Lightfoot always breeds true," and walked around the mare's hindquarters and stopped and swore out loud.

Her father laughed until he had to put a hand on her shoulder to steady himself. "You never told him not to breed her," he said, wiping his eyes.

"I never thought he'd breed her to a jackass with ears as long as his," Tom Ladd said.

The colt stopped sucking and flung his head up and stared at them. His ears were so long that they looked as if they might tip him over. He had eyes as large and dark and mournful as a Negro baby's. The fawn color about his muzzle gave him the look of a little clown. She put her arms about his furry rump and he kicked feebly, nuzzling against his mother's side.

"Hush," she said, "you'll hurt his feelings."

It was a year later that Tom Ladd had given him to her, after Jake Robinson had had to give up trying to break him.

She led the mule down the hill. The horses heard them coming and whinnied. She led him up to them, so close that they could touch noses. Then she made a halter out of the broken rope and led the three of them back to the thicket. The old mare and the horse went quietly to their places beside the big pine but Lightning kept sidestepping and shaking his head. She led him off a little way and tied him to another tree and opened the sack and gave Bess and Gray four nubbins apiece and the clover that she had gathered in the orchard. When they had finished eating she tethered them again and mounted Lightning and rode him down the ravine.

The sun had set. Here in the thick woods it was dark. But she could see the light from the house, shining through the trees. They did not use the path at all now. No use in keeping your horses hid off in the woods if there was a path leading to them. But it was hard, riding through the underbrush. She had to lie flat on the mule's back to keep from being scraped off.

At the edge of the wood she dismounted and was about to open the gate when a sound down the road made her stop, chain in hand. Somebody was walking along the road, whistling softly. She let the chain fall with a little click against the post and led Lightning back a little way into the bushes. The sound grew. The man, or whoever it was, walked steadily, whistling as he came.

She pressed close against the mule, her arm over his withers. He stood quietly but the sound of his breathing seemed to fill all the thicket. Light from the house fell in a great fan across the road. A man's visored cap and the knapsack that bulged at his shoulder showed black against it for a second and then he passed on. But the sound of his whistling was all around her still. An old tune that she had always known:

"One morning, one morning, one morning in May
I met a fair lady a-wending her way..."

She stood there until the sound had quite died away, then, lifting the chain with infinite care, she opened the gate and led the mule across the road and into the yard.

The front door opened. Her sister stood on the porch. "Barbara!" she called.

Barbara did not answer. After a little Sophy went inside and shut the door. Barbara drew Lightning swiftly through the yard and toward the stable. Halfway there she stopped. The stable wouldn't do. That was the first place they went. Nor the hen house, though it was big enough. None of the outbuildings would do. They always searched outbuildings, to make sure they didn't miss anything. They would search an outbuilding when they wouldn't search the house itself. She turned back into the yard and ran down the cellar steps, the mule lumbering behind her.

He came down the last two steps so fast that he ran over her.

She felt the impact of his chest between her shoulders and knew that his forefoot had grazed her ankle before she went sprawling down in the dark. She lay there a moment, wondering how badly she was hurt, then got to her feet and felt her way to where he stood. She stroked his neck and talked to him gently. "Poor little Lightning. Him have a hard time. Mammy *know* him have a hard time."

A ray of light struck on the wall. Sophy stood at the head of the steps, a lighted lamp in her hand. She peered down into the cellar, then came a little way down the steps, holding the lamp high over her head.

"Have you gone distracted?" she asked.

"Why don't you see after the stock?" Barbara asked coldly. "He's not hurting your old cellar."

She poured what corn was left in the sack out upon the earthen floor, fastened the cellar doors, and followed Sophy up the steps.

Her twelve-year-old brother sat beside the stove, whittling. He looked up eagerly as she came in. "You going to keep that mule in the cellar, sister? You going to keep him in there all the time?"

Barbara sat down in the big chair by the window. She lifted her skirt to examine her leg. Blood was caked on her shin and the flesh of the ankle was bruised and discolored. She felt her lips trembling. She spoke brusquely:

"I saw a soldier going past the house just as I was getting ready to cross the road."

Sophy did not seem to have heard her. "Why didn't you leave that mule out in the hollow?" she asked.

"He slipped his halter," Barbara said. "I had to walk all over the woods to find him."

"It would have been a good thing if you couldn't find him," Sophy said.

Barbara looked at her steadily. "I'm going to keep him," she said. "I don't care what you say. I'm going to keep him."

Sophy, compressing her lips, did not answer. Cummy had gone over and sat down at the kitchen table, where they always ate nowadays. "Aren't we going to have any supper?" he asked.

Sophy went out on the back porch and returned with two covered dishes. "There's some black-eyed peas," she said. "And Mrs. Thomas sent us a pat of butter. I thought we might as well have it while it was fresh."

She bent over the table, arranging knives and forks and plates. A frail woman of twenty-seven, who looked, Barbara thought suddenly, at least thirty-five. That was because she was just recovering from one of her asthmatic attacks. No, it was because she was so thin. She had never noticed until tonight how sunken her sister's temples were. And under her cheekbones, where even as a young girl she had had hollows, were deep wells of shadow.

"She can't stand it," she thought. "She's not strong like me. She can't stand it....I ought not to keep him. Those nubbins I gave him today. I could have taken them to the mill and had them ground into meal."

"There's two jars of preserves left," she said, "a jar of quince and a jar of peach."

Cummy was up from the table and halfway down the cellar steps before she had stopped speaking. He brought up the two jars.

Sophy nodded. "Might as well have them now. Preserves aren't any good without buttered bread, and no telling when we'll have butter again."

Barbara did not answer. She was looking through the open door into the hall. "Isn't that somebody on the porch?" she asked.

Cummy half rose from his chair. "You sit still," Barbara said sharply.

She got up and went through the hall toward the front door. When she was halfway there she stopped. "Who is it?" she called.

The door swung slowly open. A man stepped into the hall. A tall, red-faced man in a dark cloak and cavalryman's boots. He looked at Barbara a moment before he took off his visored cap.

"Good evening, miss," he said. "This the way to Gordonsville?"

"Yes," Barbara said, and stepped out onto the porch. "You keep on down this lane till you hit the pike. It isn't more than a quarter of a mile."

The soldier was looking back through the hall into the lighted kitchen. "How about a bite of supper?" he asked, smiling a little.

Barbara moved past him to the door. She put her hand on the knob. "I'm sorry but we haven't got a thing."

He thrust his foot swiftly forward just before the door closed. He was laughing. "That's too bad," he said, and pushed past her into the kitchen.

Sophy got up slowly from her chair. Her face had gone dead white. Her mouth was open and then it shut, quivering like a rabbit's. She was always like that. In a minute she would be crying and telling him it was all right, the way she did last spring when the soldiers took all the meat out of the smokehouse.

Barbara thought of that time and her right hand clenched in the folds of her skirt. She put the other on Sophy's shoulder and pointed to the door. "Go on," she said, "you go on and take Cummy with you."

The soldier had sat down at the table and, pulling the dish of peas toward him, looked up at her, shaking his head a little. "I'm mighty sorry," he said, "but I'm so hungry I could eat a horse." He laughed. "Horse gave out on me way back up the road. I must have walked three miles."

Barbara leaned forward until her face was on a level with his. A vein in her forehead stood out, swollen and tinged faintly with purple. She spoke through clenched teeth.

"Aren't you ashamed to take the bread out of the mouths of women and children?"

The soldier stared. He seemed about to rise from his chair, but he sank back, shaking his head again, laughing. After a moment he spoke, his mouth full of peas. "Lady, you got any pie?"

"We haven't got anything," Barbara said. "There isn't anything left on this place worth the taking. It doesn't make any difference which side they're on. They come and take everything."

The soldier nodded. A mischievous light came in his eyes. "Those damn Rebs," he said. "You turn 'em loose on a place and they'll strip it."

"Don't you say 'damn Reb' to me!" Barbara cried.

He put his knife and fork down and sat looking at her. His eyes sparkled. "Damn Reb," he said. "Damn Reb. Damn Reb....If you aren't the feistiest Reb I ever saw!"

Barbara left the room. Sophy and Cummy were on the front porch. She walked up and down a few minutes, then went into the deserted parlor and stood before one of the darkened windows. "I wish I could kill him," she said aloud. "God! I wish I could kill him."

"Hush!" came a fierce whisper. "Here he comes."

The soldier stood in the doorway. "That was a fine dinner," he said. He made a little bow. "I'm much obliged to you."

No one spoke. He lingered, fastened his cloak. He was humming that same tune.

"One morning, one morning, one morning in May
I met a fair lady a-wending her way..."

"*Very much* obliged," he said. His eyes sought Barbara's. She did
not answer, staring at Sophy, who had moved over and was lighting one
of the lamps that stood on the mantel, as if, Barbara thought, they had
come in here to entertain a welcome guest. Sophy finished lighting the
lamp and sat down on the old love seat, her hands folded in her lap.
Cummy had slipped into the room and sat down beside her. On the
mantel the lamp burned steadily, revealing objects unfamiliar from long
disuse: the walnut chairs, upholstered in faded red, the mute piano, the
damask curtains. Their mother had been proud of her parlor when all
those things were new. The soldier was looking about him as calmly as if
he had been invited to spend the evening in their company. A little smile
played about the corners of his mouth. He walked over to a whatnot in
the corner. Dresden figurines were on the top shelf and on the shelf below a hand-painted Japanese fan lay among a pile of Indian arrowheads
that Cummy had picked up on the old chipping ground. He took one in
his hand. The bits of mica embedded in the flint gleamed as he turned it
over slowly. "We get 'em like that on our home place," he said, and
looked into her eyes and smiled. "Up in Indiana." He laid the arrow-
head down and picked up a larger flint. "That's not for an arrow," he
said. "That's a sword. A ceremonial sword. My grandfather knew an
old Indian once told him what all the different kinds were."

He spoke in a low, casual tone, as if to somebody who stood beside
him, somebody who was listening and in a minute would say something
back. But there was not anybody here who would listen to anything that
he might ever say. And the room itself was not used to the sound of
human voices. There had not been anybody in it for a long time, not
since that night, two years ago, the night of Marie's wedding. They had
pushed the chairs back and danced till dawn broke at the windows. Gil
Lathrop played the fiddle. Sometimes he sang as he played:

"And the voice that I heard made the valleys all ring;
It was fairer than the music when the nightingale sings."

The soldier was humming again. That song, the song they all sang
that night, seemed to go on inside him, and now he had to have some-

thing to listen to and words rang out in the still room:

"And if ever I return it will be in the spring
For to see the waters flowing, hear the nightingale sing."

He had a clear tenor voice. At home, among his own people, he would be the one to sing at the gatherings. He picked up the little, bright-colored fan. Over its rim his eyes sought hers again. "Now which one of you ladies does this belong to?"

"For to see the waters flowing, hear the nightingale sing..."

But that night you could not tell who was singing: the song was on every lip. "Look!" Ruth Emory said. "There's Tom Ladd. I never saw him at a dance before." He would have asked me to marry him, but for all their talk. "It will be in the spring." No, I will never see him again. There are some men do not come home from a war. If the music could only have gone on that night...

The man's eyes were blue, really, not gray. Blue, overlaid with white, like frozen water. There was no song in the room now. Black pinpoints grew in his eyes, glinted as he slowly turned his head. "Now what was that?" he asked.

Barbara whirled and stood with her back to the window, her hands locked tight in front of her. She thought at first that she had not heard anything, that it was only the blood pounding in her ears. Then it came again, the slow beat-beat of the mule's hoof against the brick wall of the cellar.

She left the window and walked across the room. As she passed the fireplace she pushed the shovel with her foot. It fell to the floor with a clatter, taking the tongs with it. The Yankee picked them up and stood them on the hearth. He looked at her, his eyes grave and speculative.

"What was that?" he asked again.

She took a step toward him. "It's my brother," she said. "He's armed." She took another step. "He'll shoot you."

The Yankee laughed, cocking his head on one side. "Now what good would it do you to get me shot?"

He walked in his heavy boots out into the hall and back into the kitchen. They followed him. He lifted the lighted lantern that sat on the table and beckoned to Cummy. "Come here, son. I've got an errand for you."

Cummy's face took on its stubborn look. "I don't want to go down there," he said.

Sophy was crying. "Poor little motherless boy. Don't make him go." The Yankee put his arm about Cummy's shoulders. "You come along with me, son. Nothing's going to hurt you."

He opened the door into the cellar and, holding the lantern, leaned over Cummy's shoulder, to look down the stairs. He straightened up, laughing. "That's a mighty peculiar brother you've got down there," he said.

He handed the lantern to Cummy. "You hold on to that, son, and don't get in the way of my right arm. I wouldn't be surprised if you had another brother down there."

They started down the steps. The Yankee walked slowly, a step behind Cummy, his arm still about Cummy's shoulder. Barbara watched them until they were halfway down, then she ran out through the back door and around the side of the house.

The double cellar doors were still closed when she got there, but she could hear the Yankee fumbling with the bolt. He had pulled it out. The doors slammed back. Lightning came slowly up the steps. She waited until his head and shoulders were level with the ground before she reached up and caught the halter.

"This is my mule," she said.

Lightning snorted and tossed his head. The whites of his eyes showed. His ears were laid back. She tugged at the halter again. "You let him go," she sobbed. "You better let him go!"

The Yankee raised his arm and pushed her, so hard that she spun away from him to fall on the grass. He brought Lightning up the last two steps, then came and stood over her while she was getting to her feet. His hand was on her arm. The fingers pressed it for a moment, the firm, friendly, admonitory pressure a man might give your arm—at a dance, if there was some secret understanding between you that he wanted to remind you of. "I didn't mean to hurt you," he said, "but you oughtn't to have come interfering. Between us we might have broken that mule's legs on those steps."

She didn't answer, staring past him at the mule where he stood in the wash of light from the window, gazing before him out of great, dark eyes. His coat and his little bristling mane shone red in the light. His nostrils were ringed with palest fawn color. If she went over now and cupped his nose in her hands, the nostrils, snuffling gently in and out, would beat against her palm like butterflies' wings.

She looked up into gray eyes that sparkled in the light. The soldier had a broad mouth that slanted a little to one side. The blunt lips seemed always just about to stretch into a smile. She looked away, thinking how you could set your thumbs at the corners of those lips and rend the mouth from side to side and then, grasping in your hands the head—the head that you have severed from the body—you would beat it up and down on the boards of the well sweep until you cast it, a battered bloody pulp, into those grasses that sprang up there beside the well.

She walked over and sat down on the wooden platform. The planks were cool and wet. She gripped them hard with both hands. The man was still there, making a throat latch out of a piece of twine. He was turning around. "You haven't got a bridle to spare, Bud?"

Cummy spoke up shrilly. "You better not take that mule. I'm telling you now. You better not take him. Can't anybody do anything with him but Tom Ladd and he's joined the army."

The Yankee had thrown a leg over Lightning's back and was sitting there looking down at them. "I'm swapping you a good mare for this mule," he said. "She gave out on me...About three miles up the road..."

Lightning had stood quiet while the man mounted but he reared suddenly and plunged forward, his small, wicked head tucked down, his ears flat on his neck. And now he plunged on, turned the corner into the lane, and broke into a mad gallop. The soldier's voice drifted back above the pounding of hooves. "I'd be glad for you to have her...Lying down under a big oak...About three miles up the road."

Cummy caught hold of Barbara's arm. "Come on, sister. Let's go see if we can find that mare."

Barbara did not move. Cummy waited a moment, and sat down beside her. "One thing," he said, "he won't ever get Lightning through those woods. Lightning'll rub him off on the branches."

Barbara had been sitting with her head lifted, staring off into the lane. When he began to speak again she raised her hand. "Hush!" she said sharply and then: "What's that?"

Cummy jumped to his feet. "It's that Yankee," he said. "He's in trouble."

He bounded across the yard and through the open gate. Barbara followed him. It was black dark in the lane. They could not see their hands before them. There was no sound except the thudding of their own feet and then it came again, the cry which rose and swelled and broke finally into hideous shrieks. Barbara caught up with Cummy and pulled him to the left. "It's this way," she panted, "over in the woods."

They crashed through the underbrush and came out in a little glade. They could not see anything at first, then they made out the white trunk of a sycamore and beside it, Lightning, stock-still under a low-hanging bough, his head sharply lifted, his forefeet planted wide apart. The dark mass between his spread legs was too dense for shadow.

Cummy was holding on to Barbara's hand. "Somebody's coming," he whispered.

Barbara did not look around. "It's Sis Sophy," she said. "She's bringing the lantern."

She stood motionless. The long rays of the lantern flickered across the tree trunk and fell on the soldier's face, on the place where his eyes had been, on the blood that oozed from the torn mouth onto the dead leaves.

Sophy was whimpering softly. The lantern shook in her hand. "We'll have to bury him...We'll have to get somebody to help us bury him."

Barbara's eyes came away from the dead man to rest on Sophy's face. "I'm not going to help bury him," she said.

She walked past Sophy to where the mule stood. She put her hand up and cupped it over his quivering nostrils. He gave a long sigh and stepped clear of the body. She slid her arm down to rest on his withers.

"Come on," she said, "let's go home."

A Woman

Rose Terry Cooke

"Not perfect, nay! but full of tender wants."
—The Princess

I SAT BY my window sewing, one bright autumn day, thinking much of twenty other things, and very little of the long seam that slipped away from under my fingers slowly, but steadily, when I heard the front-door open with a quick push, and directly into my open door entered Laura Lane, with a degree of impetus that explained the previous sound in the hall. She threw herself into a chair before me, flung her hat on the floor, threw her shawl across the window-sill, and looked at me without speaking: in fact, she was quite too much out of breath to speak.

I was used to Laura's impetuousness; so I only smiled and said, "Good morning."

"Oh!" said Laura, with a long breath, "I have got something to tell you, Sue."

"That's nice," said I; "news is worth double here in the country; tell me slowly, to prolong the pleasure."

"You must guess first. I want to have you try your powers for once; guess, do!"

"Mr. Lincoln defeated?"

"Oh, no,—at least not that I know of; all the returns from this State are not in yet, of course not from the others; besides, do you think I'd make such a fuss about politics?"

"You might," said I, thinking of all the beautiful and brilliant women that in other countries and other times had made "fuss" more potent than Laura's about politics.

"But I shouldn't," retorted she.

"Then there is a new novel out?"

"No!" (with great indignation).

"Or the parish have resolved to settle Mr. Hermann?"

"How stupid you are, Sue! Everybody knew that yesterday."

"But I am not everybody."

"I shall have to help you, I see," sighed Laura, half provoked. "Somebody is going to be married."

"'Mademoiselle, the great Mademoiselle!'"

Laura stared at me. I ought to have remembered she was eighteen, and not likely to have read Sevigne. I began more seriously, laying down my seam.

"Is it anybody I know, Laura?"

"Of course, or you wouldn't care about it, and it would be no fun to tell you."

"Is it you?"

Laura grew indignant.

"Do you think I should bounce in, in this way, to tell you *I* was engaged?"

"Why not? shouldn't you be happy about it?"

"Well, if I were, I should"—

Laura dropped her beautiful eyes and colored.

"The thoughts of youth are long, long thoughts."

I am sure she felt as much strange, sweet shyness sealing her girlish lips at that moment as when she came, very slowly and silently, a year after, to tell me she was engaged to Mr. Hermann. I had to smile and sigh both.

"Tell me, then, Laura; for I cannot guess."

"I'll tell you the gentleman's name, and perhaps you can guess the lady's then: it is Frank Addison."

"Frank Addison!" echoed I, in surprise; for this young man was one I knew and loved well, and I could not think who in our quiet village had sufficient attraction for his fastidious taste.

He was certainly worth marrying, though he had some faults, being as proud as was endurable, as shy as a child, and altogether endowed with a full appreciation, to say the least, of his own charms and merits: but he was sincere, and loyal, and tender; well cultivated, yet not priggish or pedantic; brave, well-bred, and high-principled; handsome besides. I knew him thoroughly; I had held him on my lap, fed him with sugar-plums, soothed his child-sorrows, and scolded his naughtiness, many a time; I had stood with him by his mother's dying bed and consoled him by my own tears, for his mother I loved dearly; so, ever since, Frank had been both near and dear to me, for a mutual sorrow is a tie that may bind together even a young man and an old maid in close and kindly friendship. I was the more surprised at his engagement because I thought he would have been the first to tell me of it; but I reflected that Laura was his cousin, and relationship has an etiquette of precedence above any other social link.

"Yes,—Frank Addison! Now guess, Miss Sue! for he is not here to tell you,—he is in New York; and here in my pocket I have got a letter for you, but you sha'n't have it till you have well guessed."

I was—I am ashamed to confess it—but I was not a little comforted at hearing of that letter. One may shake up a woman's heart with every alloy of life, grind, break, scatter it, till scarce a throb of its youth beats there, but to its last bit it is feminine still; and I felt a sudden sweetness of relief to know that my boy had not forgotten me.

"I don't know whom to guess, Laura; who ever marries after other people's fancy? If I were to guess Sally Hetheridge, I might come as near as I shall to the truth."

Laura laughed.

"You know better," said she. "Frank Addison is the last man to marry a dried-up old tailoress."

"I don't know that he is; according to his theories of women and marriage, Sally would make him happy. She is true-hearted, I am sure,—generous, kind, affectionate, sensible, and poor. Frank has always raved about the beauty of the soul, and the degradation of marrying money,—therefore, Laura, I believe he is going to marry a beauty and an heiress. I guess Josephine Bowen."

"Susan!" exclaimed Laura, with a look of intense astonishment, "how could you guess it?"

"Then it is she?"

"Yes, it is,—and I am so sorry! such a childish, giggling, silly little creature! I can't think how Frank could fancy her; she is just like Dora in *David Copperfield*—a perfect gosling! I am as vexed"—

"But she is exquisitely pretty."

"Pretty! well, that is all; he might as well have bought a nice picture, or a dolly! I am all out of patience with Frank. I haven't the heart to congratulate him."

"Don't be unreasonable, Laura; when you get as old as I am, you will discover how much better and greater facts are than theories. It's all very well for men to say,—

Beauty is unripe childhood's cheat,—

the soul is all they love,—the fair, sweet character, the lofty mind, the tender woman's heart, and gentle loveliness; but when you come down to the statistics of love and matrimony, you find Sally Hetheridge at sixty an old maid, and Miss Bowen at nineteen adored by a dozen men and engaged to one. No, Laura, if I had ten sisters, and a fairy godmother for each, I should request that ancient dame to endow them all with beauty and silliness, sure that then they would achieve a woman's best destiny,—a home."

Laura's face burned indignantly; she hardly let me finish before she exclaimed,—

"Susan Lee! I am ashamed of you! here are you, an old maid, as happy as anybody, decrying all good gifts to a woman, except beauty, because, indeed, they stand in the way of her marriage! as if a woman was only made to be a housekeeper!"

Laura's indignation amused me. I went on,—

"Yes, I am happy enough; but I should have been much happier, had I married. Don't waste your indignation, dear; you are pretty enough to excuse your being sensible, and you ought to agree with my ideas, because they excuse Frank, and yours do not."

"I don't want to excuse him; I am really angry about it. I can't bear to have Frank throw himself away; she is pretty now, but what will she be in ten years?"

"People in love do not usually enter into such remote calculations; love is today's delirium; it has an element of divine faith in it, in not caring for the morrow. But, Laura, we can't help this matter, and we have neither of us any conscience involved in it. Miss Bowen may be better than we know. At any rate, Frank is happy, and that ought to satisfy both you and me just now."

Laura's eyes filled with tears. I could see them glisten on the dark lashes, as she affected to tie her hat, all the time untying it as fast as ever the knot slid. She was a sympathetic little creature, and loved Frank very sincerely, having known him as long as she could remember. She gave me a silent kiss, and went away, leaving the letter, yet unopened, lying in my lap. I did not open it just then. I was thinking of Josephine Bowen.

Every summer, for three years, Mr. and Mrs. Bowen had come to Ridgefield for country-air, bringing with them their adopted daughter, whose baptismal name had resigned in favor of the pet appellation "Kitten,"—a name better adapted to her nature and aspect than the *Imperatrice* appellation that belonged to her. She was certainly as charming a little creature as ever one saw in flesh and blood. Her sweet child's-face, her dimpled, fair cheeks, her rose-bud of a mouth, and great, wistful, blue eyes, that laughed like flax-flowers in a south-wind, her tiny, round chin, and low, white forehead, were all adorned by profuse rings and coils and curls of true gold-yellow, that never would grow long, or be braided, or stay smooth, or do anything but ripple and twine and push their shining tendrils out of every bonnet or hat or hood the little creature wore, like a stray parcel of sunbeams that would shine. Her delicate, tiny figure was as round as a child's,—her funny hands as quaint as some fat baby's, with short fingers and dimpled knuckles. She was a creature as much made to be petted as a King-Charles spaniel,— and petted she was, far beyond any possibility of a crumpled rose-leaf. Mrs. Bowen was fat, loving, rather foolish, but the best of friends and the poorest of enemies; she wanted everybody to be happy, and fat, and well as she was, and would urge the necessity of wine, and entire idleness, and horse-exercise, upon a poor minister, just as honestly and energetically as if he could have afforded them; an idea to the contrary never crossed her mind spontaneously; but, if introduced there, brought forth direct results of bottles, bank-bills, and loans of ancient horses, only to be checked by friendly remonstrance, or the suggestion that a poor man might be also proud. Mr. Bowen was tall and spare, a man of much sense and shrewd kindliness, but altogether subject and submissive to "Kitten's" slightest wish. She never wanted anything; no princess in a story-book had less to desire; and this entire spoiling and indulgence seemed to her only the natural course of things. She took it as an open rose takes sunshine, with so much simplicity, and heartiness, and beaming content, and perfume of sweet, careless affection, that she was not given over to any little vanities or affectations, but was always a dear, good little child, as happy as the day was long, and quite without a fear or apprehension. I had seen very little of her in those three summers, for I had been away at the sea-side, trying to fan the flickering life that alone was left to me with pungent salt breezes and stinging baptisms of spray, but I had liked that little pretty well. I did not think her so silly as Laura did: she seemed to me so purely simple, that I sometimes wondered if her honest directness and want of guile were folly or not. But I liked to see her, as she cantered past my door on her pony, the gold tendrils thick clustered about her throat and under the brim of her black hat, and her bright blue eyes sparkling with the keen air, and a real wild-rose bloom on her smiling face. She was a prettier sight even than my profuse chrysanthemums, whose masses of garnet and yellow and white nodded languidly to the autumn winds to-day.

I recalled myself from this dream of recollection, better satisfied with Miss Bowen than I had been before. I could see just how her beauty had bewitched Frank,—so bright, so tiny, so loving: one always wants to gather a little, gay, odor-breathing rose-bud for one's own, and such she was to him.

So then I opened his letter. It was dry and stiff: men's letters almost always are; they cannot say what they feel; they will be fluent of statistics, or description, or philosophy, or politics, but as to feeling,—there they are dumb, except in real love-letters, and, of course, Frank's was unsatisfactory accordingly. Once, toward the end, came out a natural sentence: "Oh, Sue! if you knew her, you wouldn't wonder!" So he had, after all, felt the apology he would not speak; he had some little deference left for his deserted theories.

Well I knew what touched his pride, and struck that little revealing spark from his deliberate pen: Josephine Bowen was rich, and he only a poor lawyer in a country-town: he felt it even in this first flush of love, and to that feeling I must answer when I wrote him,—not merely to the announcement, and the delight, and the man's pride. So I answered his letter at once, and he answered mine in person. I had nothing to say to him, when I saw him; it was enough to see how perfectly happy and contented he was,—how the proud, restless eyes, that had always looked a challenge to all the world, were now tranquil to their depths. Nothing had interfered with his passion. Mrs. Bowen liked him always, Mr. Bowen liked him now; nobody had objected, it had not occurred to anybody to object; money had not been mentioned any more than it would have been in Arcadia. Strange to say, the good, simple woman, and the good, shrewd man had both divined Frank's peculiar sensitiveness, and respected it.

There was no period fixed for the engagement, it was indefinite as yet, and the winter, with all its excitements of South and North, passed by at length, and the first of April the Bowens moved out to Ridgefield. It was earlier than usual; but the city was crazed with excitement, and Mr. Bowen was tired and worn; he wanted quiet. Then I saw a great deal of Josephine, and in spite of Laura, and her still restless objections to the child's childish, laughing, inconsequent manner, I grew into liking her: not that there seemed any great depth to her; she was not specially intellectual, or witty, or studious, or practical; she did not try to be anything: perhaps that was her charm to me. I had seen so many women laboring at themselves to be something, that one who was content to live without thinking about it was a real phenomenon to me. Nothing bores me (though I be stoned for the confession, I must make it!) more than a woman who is bent on improving her mind, or forming her manners, or moulding her character, or watching her motives, with that deadly-lively conscientiousness that makes so many good people disagreeable. Why can't they consider the lilies, which grow by receiving sun and air and dew from God, and not hopping about over the lots to find the warmest corner or the wettest hollow, to see how much bigger and brighter they can grow? It was real rest to me to have this tiny, bright creature come in to me every day during Frank's office-hours and unintentionally as a yellow butterfly would come in at the window. Sometimes she strayed to the kitchen-porch, and, resting her elbows on the window-sill and her chin on both palms, looked at me with wondering eyes while I made bread or cake; sometimes she came by the long parlor-window, and sat down on a *brioche* at my feet while I sewed, talking in her direct, unconsidered way, so fresh, and withal so good and pure, I came to thinking the day very dull that did not bring "Kitten" to see me.

The nineteenth of April, in the evening, my door opened again with an impetuous bang; but this time it was Frank Addison, his eyes blazing, his dark cheek flushed, his whole aspect fired and furious.

"Good God, Sue! do you know what they've done in Baltimore?"

"What?" said I, in vague terror, for I had been an alarmist from the first: I had once lived at the South.

"Fired on a Massachusetts regiment, and killed—nobody knows how many yet; but killed, and wounded."

I could not speak: it was the lighted train of a powder-magazine burning before my eyes. Frank began to walk up and down the room.

"I must go! I must! I must!" came involuntarily from his working lips.

"Frank! Frank! remember Josephine."

It was a cowardly thing to do, but I did it. Frank turned ghastly white, and sat down in a chair opposite me. I had, for the moment, quenched his ardor; he looked at me with anxious eyes, and drew a long sigh, almost a groan.

"Josephine!" he said, as if the name were new to him, so vitally did the idea seize all his faculties.

"Well, dear!" said a sweet little voice at the door.

Frank turned, and seemed to see a ghost; for there in the door-way stood "Kitten," her face perhaps a shade calmer than ordinary, swinging in one hand the tasselled hood she wore of an evening, and holding her shawl together with the other. Over her head we discerned the spare, upright shape of Mr. Bowen, looking grim and penetrative, but not unkindly.

"What is the matter?" went on the little lady.

Nobody answered, but Frank and I looked at each other. She came in now and went toward him, Mr. Bowen following at a respectful distance, as if he were her footman.

"I've been looking for you everywhere," said she, with the slightest possible suggestion of reserve, or perhaps timidity, in her voice. "Father went first for me, and when you were not at Laura's, or the office, or the post-office, or Mrs. Sledge's, then I knew you were here; so I came with him, because—because"—she hesitated the least bit here—"we love Sue."

Frank still looked at her with his soul in his eyes, as if he wanted to absorb her utterly into himself and then die. I never saw such a look before; I hope I never may again; it haunts me to this day.

I can pause now to recall and reason about the curious, exalted atmosphere that seemed suddenly to have surrounded us, as if bare spirits communed there, not flesh and blood. Frank did not move; he sat and looked at her standing near him, so near that her shawl trailed against his chair; but presently when she wanted to grasp something, she moved aside and took hold of another chair,—not his: it was a little thing, but it interpreted her.

"Well?" said he, in a hoarse tone.

Just then she moved, as I said, and laid one hand on the back of a chair: it was the only symptom of emotion she showed; her voice was as childish-clear and steady as before.

"You want to go, Frank, and I thought you would rather be married to me first; so I came to find you and tell you I would."

Frank sprang to his feet like a shot man; I cried; Josephine stood looking at us quite steadily, her head a little bent toward me, her eyes calm, but very wide open; and Mr. Bowen gave an audible grunt. I suppose the right thing for Frank to have done in any well-regulated novel would have been to fall on his knees and call her all sorts of names; but people never do—that is, any people that I knew—just what the gentlemen in novels do; so he walked off and looked out of the window. To my aid came the goddess of slang. I stopped snuffling directly.

"Josephine," said I, solemnly, "you are a brick!"

"Well, I should think so!" said Mr. Bowen, slightly sarcastic.

Josey laughed very softly. Frank came back from the window, and then the three went off together, she holding by her father's arm, Frank on his other side. I could not but look after them as I stood in the hall-door, and then I came back and sat down to read the paper Frank had flung on the floor when he came in. It diverted my mind enough from myself to enable me to sleep; for I was burning with self-disgust to think of my cowardice,—I, a grown woman, supposed to be more than ordinarily strong-minded by some people, fairly shamed and routed by a girl Laura Lane called "Dora"!

In the morning, Frank came directly after breakfast. He had found his tongue now, certainly,—for words seemed no way to satisfy him, talking of Josephine; and presently she came, too, as brave and bright as ever, sewing busily on a long housewife for Frank; and after her, Mrs. Bowen, making a huge pin-ball in red, white, and blue, and full of the trunk she was packing for Frank to carry, to be filled with raspberry-jam, hard gingerbread, old brandy, clove-cordial, guava-jelly, strong peppermints, quinine, black cake, cod-liver oil, horehound-candy, Brandreth's pills, damson-leather, and cherry-pectoral, packed in with flannel and cotton bandages, lint, lancets, old linen, and cambric handkerchiefs.

I could not help laughing, and was about to remonstrate, when Frank shook his head at me from behind her. He said afterward he let her go on that way, because it kept her from crying over Josephine. As for the trunk, he should give it to Miss Dix as soon as ever he reached Washington.

In a week, Frank had got his commission as captain of a company in a volunteer regiment; he went into camp at Dartford, our chief town, and set to work in earnest at tactics and drill. The Bowens also went to Dartford, and the last week in May came back for Josey's wedding. I am a superstitious creature,—most women are,—and it went to my heart to have them married in May; but I did not say so, for it seemed imperative, as the regiment were to leave for Washington in June, early.

The day but one before the wedding was one of those warm, soft days that so rarely come in May. My windows were open, and the faint scent of springing grass and opening blossoms came in on every southern breath of wind. Josey had brought her work over to sit beside me. She was hemming her wedding-veil,—a long cloud of *tulle;* and as she sat there, pinching the frail stuff in her fingers, and handling her needle with such deft little ways, as if they were old friends and understood each other, there was something so youthful, so unconscious, so wistfully sweet in her aspect, I could not believe her the same resolute, brave creature I had seen that night in April.

"Josey," said I, "I don't know how you can be willing to let Frank go."

It was a hard thing for me to say, and I said it without thinking. She leaned back in her chair, and pinched her hem faster than ever.

"I don't know, either," said she. "I suppose it was because I ought. I don't think I am so willing now, Sue: it was easy at first, for I was so angry and grieved about those Massachusetts men; but now, when I get time to think, I do ache over it! I never let him know; for it is just the same right now, and he thinks so. Besides, I never let myself grieve much, even to myself, lest he might find it out. I must keep bright till he goes. It would be so very hard on him, Susy, to think I was crying at home."

I said no more,—I could not; and happily for me, Frank came in with a bunch of wild-flowers, that Josey took with a smile as gay as the columbines, and a blush that outshone the "pinkster-bloomjes," as our old Dutch "chore-man" called the wild honeysuckle. A perfect shower of dew fell from them all over her wedding-veil.

The day of her marriage was showery as April, but a gleam of soft, fitful sunshine streamed into the little church windows, and fell across the tiny figure that stood by Frank Addison's side, like a ray of glory, till the golden curls glittered through her veil, and the fresh lilies-of-the-valley that crowned her hair and ornamented her simple dress seemed to send out a fresher fragrance, and glow with more pearly whiteness. Mrs. Bowen, in a square pew, sobbed, and snuffled, and sopped her eyes with a lace pocket-handkerchief, and spilt cologne all over her dress, and mashed the flowers on her French hat against the dusty pew-rail, and behaved generally like a hen that has lost her sole chicken. Mr. Bowen sat upright in the pew-corner, uttering sonorous hems, whenever his wife sobbed audibly; he looked as dry as a stick, and as grim as Bunyan's giant, and chewed cardamom-seeds, as if he were a ruminating animal.

After the wedding came lunch; it was less formal than dinner, and nobody wanted to sit down before hot dishes and go through with the accompanying ceremonies. For my part, I always did hate gregarious eating: it is well enough for animals, in pasture or pen; but a thing that has so little that is graceful or dignified about it as this taking food, especially as the thing is done here in America, ought, in my opinion, to be a solitary act. I never bring my quinine and iron to my friends and invite them to share it; why should I ask them to partake of my beef, mutton, and pork, with the accompanying mastication, the distortion of face, and the suppings and gulpings of fluid dishes that many respectable people indulge in? No,—let me, at least, eat alone. But I did not do so to-day; for Josey, with the most unsentimental air of hunger, sat down at the table and ate two sandwiches, three pickled mushrooms, a piece of pie, and a glass of jelly, with a tumbler of ale besides. Laura Lane sat on the other side of the table, her great dark eyes intently fixed on

Josephine, and a look in which wonder was delicately shaded with disgust quivering about her mouth. She was a feeling soul, and thought a
girl in love ought to live on strawberries, honey, and spring-water. I
believe she really doubted Josey's affection for Frank, when she saw her
eat a real mortal meal on her wedding-day. As for me, I am a poor,
miserable, unhealthy creature, not amenable to ordinary dietetic rules,
and much given to taking any excitement, above a certain amount in lieu
of rational food; so I sustained myself on a cup of coffee, and saw Frank
also make tolerable play of knife and fork, though he did take some
blanc-mange with his cold chicken, and profusely peppered his
Charlotte-Russe!

Mrs. Bowen alternately wept and ate pie. Mr. Bowen said the jelly
tasted of turpentine, and the chickens must have gone on Noah's voy-
age, they were so tough; he growled at the ale, and asked nine questions
about the coffee, all of a derogatory sort, and never once looked at
Josephine, who looked at him every time he was particularly cross, with
a rosy little smile, as if she knew why! The few other people present
behaved after the ordinary fashion; and when we had finished, Frank
and Josephine, Mr. and Mrs. Bowen, Laura Lane and I, all took the
train for Dartford. Laura was to stay two weeks, and I till the regiment
left.

An odd time I had, after we were fairly settled in our quiet hotel,
with those two girls. Laura was sentimental, sensitive, rather high-
flown, very shy, and self-conscious; it was not in her to understand Josey
at all. We had a great deal of shopping to do, as our little bride had put
off buying most of her finery till this time, on account of the few weeks
between the fixing of her marriage-day and its arrival. It was pretty
enough to see the *naive* vanity with which she selected her dresses and
shawls and laces,—the quite inconsiderate way in which she spent her
money on whatever she wanted. One day we were in a dry-goods' shop,
looking at silks; among them lay one of Marie-Louise blue,—a plain
silk, rich from its heavy texture only, soft, thick, and perfect in color.

"I will have that one," said Josephine, after she had eyed it a moment, with her head on one side, like a canary-bird. "How much is it?"

"Two-fifty a yard, Miss," said the spruce clerk, with an inaccessible
air.

"I shall look so nice in it!" Josey murmured. "Sue, will seventeen
yards do? it must be very full and long; I can't wear flounces."

"Yes, that's plenty," said I, scarce able to keep down a smile at Laura's face.

She would as soon have smoked a cigar on the steps of the hotel as have mentioned before anybody, much less a supercilious clerk, that she should "look so nice" in anything. Josey never thought of anything beyond the fact, which was only a fact. So, after getting another dress of a lavender tint, still self-colored, but corded and rich, because it went well with her complexion, and a black one, that "father liked to see against her yellow wig, as he called it," Mrs. Josephine proceeded to a milliner's, where, to Laura's further astonishment, she bought bonnets for herself, as if she had been her own doll, with an utter disregard of proper self-depreciation, trying one after another, and discarding them for various personal reasons, till at last she fixed on a little gray straw, trimmed with gray ribbon and white daisies, "for camp," she said, and another of white lace, a fabric calculated to wear twice, perhaps, if its floating sprays of clematis did not catch in any parasol on its first appearance. She called me to see how becoming both the bonnets were, viewed herself in various ways in the glass, and at last announced that she looked prettiest in the straw, but the lace was most elegant. To this succeeded purchases of lace and shawls, that still farther opened Laura's eyes, and made her face grave. She confided to me privately, that, after all, I must allow Josephine was silly and extravagant. I had just come from that little lady's room, where she sat surrounded by the opened parcels, saying, with the gravity of a child,—

"I do like pretty things, Sue! I like them more now than I used to, because Frank likes me. I am so glad I'm pretty!"

I don't know how it was, but I could not quite coincide with Laura's strictures. Josey was extravagant, to be sure; she was vain; but something so tender and feminine flavored her very faults that they charmed me. I was not an impartial judge; and I remembered, through all, that April night, and the calm, resolute, self-poised character that invested the lovely, girlish face with such dignity, strength, and simplicity. No, she was not silly; I could not grant that to Laura.

Every day we drove to the camp, and brought Frank home to dinner. Now and then he stayed with us till the next day, and even Laura could not wonder at his "infatuation," as she had once called it, when she saw how thoroughly Josephine forgot herself in her utter devotion to him; over this, Laura's eyes filled with sad forebodings.

"If anything should happen to him, Sue, it will kill her," she said. "She never can lose him and live. Poor little thing! how could Mr. Bowen let her marry him?"

"Mr. Bowen lets her do much as she likes, Laura, and always has, I imagine."

"Yes, she has been a spoiled child, I know, but it is such a pity!"

"*Has* she been spoiled? I believe, as a general thing, more children are spoiled by what the Scotch graphically call 'nagging' than by indulgence. What do you think Josey would have been, if Mrs. Brooks had been her mother?"

"I don't know, quite; unhappy, I am sure; for Mrs. Brooks's own children look as if they had been fed on chopped catechism, and whipped early every morning, ever since they were born. I never went there without hearing one or another of them told to sit up, or sit down, or keep still, or let their aprons alone, or read their Bibles; and Joe Brooks confided to me in Sunday-school that he called Deacon Smith 'old bald-head,' one day, in the street, to see if a bear wouldn't come and eat him up, he was so tired of being a good boy!"

"That's a case in point, I think, Laura, but what a jolly little boy! he ought to have a week to be naughty in, directly."

"He never will, while his mother owns a rod!" said she, emphatically.

I had beguiled Laura from her subject; for, to tell the truth, it was one I did not dare to contemplate; it oppressed and distressed me too much.

After Laura went home, we stayed in Dartford only a week, and then followed the regiment to Washington. We had been there but a few days, before it was ordered into service. Frank came into my room one night to tell me.

"We must be off to-morrow, Sue,—and you must take her back to Ridgefield at once. I can't have her here. I have told Mr. Bowen. If we should be beaten,—and we may,—raw troops may take a panic, or may fight like veterans,—but if we should run, they will make a bee-line for Washington. I should go mad to have her here with a possibility of Rebel invasion. She must go; there is no question."

He walked up and down the room, then came back and looked me straight in the face.

"Susan, if I never come back, you will be her good friend, too?"

"Yes," said I, meeting his eye as coolly as it met mine: I had learned a lesson of Josey. "I shall see you in the morning?"

"Yes"; and so he went back to her.

Morning came. Josephine was as bright, as calm, as natural, as the June day itself. She insisted on fastening "her Captain's" straps on his shoulders, purloined his cumbrous pin-ball and put it out of sight, and kept even Mrs. Bowen's sobs in subjection by the intense serenity of her manner. The minutes seemed to go like beats of a fever-pulse; ten o'clock smote on a distant bell; Josephine had retreated, as if accidentally, to a little parlor of her own, opening from our common sitting-room. Frank shook hands with Mr. Bowen; kissed Mrs. Bowen dutifully, and cordially too; gave me one strong clasp in his arms, and one kiss; then went after Josephine. I closed the door softly behind him. In five minutes by the ticking clock he came out, and strode through the room without a glance at either of us. I had heard her say "Good bye" in her sweet, clear tone, just as he opened the door; but some instinct impelled me to go in to her at once: she lay in a dead faint on the floor.

We left Washington that afternoon, and went straight back to Ridgefield. Josey was in and out of my small house continually: but for her father and mother, I think she would have stayed with me from choice. Rare letters came from Frank, and were always reported to me, but, of course, never shown. If there was any change in her manner, it was more steadily affectionate to her father and mother than ever; the fitful, playful ways of her girlhood were subdued, but, except to me, she showed no symptom of pain, no shadow of apprehension: with me alone she sometimes drooped and sighed. Once she laid her little head on my neck, and, holding me to her tightly, half sobbed,—

"Oh, I wish—I wish I could see him just for once!"

I could not speak to answer her.

As rumors of a march toward Manassas increased, Mr. and Mrs. Bowen took her to Dartford: there was no telegraph-line to Ridgefield, and but one daily mail, and now a day's delay of news might be a vital loss. I could not go with them; I was too ill. At last came that dreadful day of Bull Run. Its story of shame and blood, trebly exaggerated, ran like fire through the land. For twenty-four long hours every heart in Ridgefield seemed to stand still; then there was the better news of fewer dead than the first report, and we knew that the enemy had retreated, but no particulars. Another long, long day, and the papers said Colonel ———'s regiment was cut to pieces; the fourth mail told another story: the regiment was safe, but Captains Addison, Black, and—Jones, I think, were missing. The fifth day brought me a letter from Mr. Bowen. Frank was dead, shot through the heart, before the panic began, cheering on his men; he had fallen in the very front rank, and his gallant company, at the risk of their lives, after losing half their number as wounded or killed, had brought off his body, and carried it with them in retreat, to find at last that they had ventured all this for a lifeless corpse! He did not mention Josephine, but asked me to come to them at once, as he was obliged to go to Washington. I could not, for I was too ill to travel without a certainty of being quite useless at my journey's end. I could but just sit up. Five days after, I had an incoherent sobbing sort of letter from Mrs. Bowen, to say that they had arranged to have the funeral at Ridgefield the next day but one,—that Josephine would come out, with her, the night before, and directly to my house, if I was able to receive them. I sent word by the morning's mail that I was able, and went myself to the station to meet them.

They had come alone, and Josey preceded her mother into the little room, as if she were impatient to have any meeting with a fresh face over. She was pale as any pale blossom of spring, and as calm. Her curls, tucked away under the widow's cap she wore, and clouded by the mass of crape that shrouded her, left only a narrow line of gold above the dead quiet of her brow. Her eyes were like the eyes of a sleep-walker: they seemed to see, but not to feel sight. She smiled mechanically, and put a cold hand into mine. For any outward expression of emotion, one might have thought Mrs. Bowen the widow: her eyes were bloodshot and swollen, her nose was red, her lips tremulous, her whole face stained and washed with tears, and the skin seemed wrinkled by their salt floods. She had cried herself sick,—more over Josephine than Frank, as was natural.

It was but a short drive over to my house, but an utterly silent one. Josephine made no sort of demonstration, except that she stooped to pat my great dog as we went in. I gave her a room that opened out of mine, and put Mrs. Bowen by herself. Twice in the night I stole in to look at her: both times I found her waking, her eyes fixed on the open window, her face set in its unnatural quiet; she smiled, but did not speak. Mrs. Bowen told me in the morning that she had neither shed a tear nor slept since the news came ; it seemed to strike her at once into this cold silence, and so she had remained. About ten, a carriage was sent over from the village to take them to the funeral. This miserable custom of ours, that demands the presence of women at such ceremonies, Mrs. Bowen was the last person to evade; and when I suggested to Josey that she should stay at home with me, she looked surprised, and said, quietly, but emphatically, "Oh, no!"

After they were gone, I took my shawl and went out on the lawn. There was a young pine dense enough to shield me from the sun, sitting under which I could see the funeral procession as it wound along the river's edge up toward the burying-ground, a mile beyond the station. But there was no sun to trouble me; cool gray clouds brooded ominously over all the sky; a strong south-wind cried, and wailed, and swept in wild gusts through the woods, while in its intervals a dreadful quiet brooded over earth and heaven,—over the broad weltering river, that, swollen by recent rain, washed the green grass shores with sullen flood,—over the heavy masses of oak and hickory trees that hung on the farther hill-side,—over the silent village and its gathering people. The engine-shriek was borne on the coming wind from far down the valley. There was an air of hushed expectation and regret in Nature itself that seemed to fit the hour to its event.

Soon I saw the crowd about the station begin to move, and presently the funeral-bell swung out its solemn tones of lamentation; its measured, lingering strokes, mingled with the woful shrieking of the wind and the sighing of the pine-tree overhead, made a dirge of inexpressible force and melancholy. A weight of grief seemed to settle on my very breath: it was not real sorrow; for, though I knew it well, I had not felt yet that Frank was dead,—it was not real to me,—I could not take to my stunned perceptions the fact that he was gone. It is the protest of Nature, dimly conscious of her original eternity, against this interruption of death, that it should always be such an interruption, so incredible, so surprising, so new. No,—the anguish that oppressed me now was not the true anguish of loss, but merely the effect of these adjuncts; the pain of want, of separation, of reaching out in vain after that which is gone, of vivid dreams and tearful waking,—all this lay in wait for the future, to be still renewed, still suffered and endured, till time should be no more. Let all these pangs of recollection attest it,—these involuntary bursts of longing for the eyes that are gone and the voice that is still,—these recoils of baffled feeling seeking for the one perfect sympathy forever fled,—these pleasures dimmed in their first resplendence for want of one whose joy would have been keener and sweeter to us than our own,—these bitter sorrows crying like children in pain for the heart that should have soothed and shared them! No,—there is no such dreary lie as that which prates of consoling Time! You who are gone, if in heaven you know how we mortals fare, you know that life took from you no love, no faith,—that bitterer tears fall for you to-day than ever wet your new graves,—that the gayer words and the recalled smiles are only like the flowers that grow above you, symbols of the deeper roots we strike in your past existence,—that to the true soul there is no such thing as forgetfulness, no such mercy as diminishing regret!

Slowly the long procession wound up the river,—here, black with plumed hearse and sable mourners,—there, gay with regimental band and bright uniforms,—no stately, proper funeral, ordered by custom and marshalled by propriety, but a straggling array of vehicles: here, the doctor's old chaise,—there, an open wagon, a dusty buggy, a long, open omnibus, such as the village-stable kept for pleasure-parties or for parties of mourning who wanted to go *en masse.*

All that knew Frank, in or about Ridgefield, and all who had sons or brothers in the army, swarmed to do him honor; and the quaint, homely array crept slowly through the valley, to the sound of tolling bell and moaning wind and the low rush of the swollen river,—the first taste of war's desolation that had fallen upon us, the first dark wave of a whelming tide!

As it passed out of sight, I heard the wheels cease, one by one, their crunch and grind on the gravelled road up the slope of the grave-yard. I knew they had reached that hill-side where the dead of Ridgefield lie calmer than its living; and presently the long-drawn notes of that hymn-tune consecrated to such occasions—old China—rose and fell in despairing cadences on my ear. If ever any music was invented for the express purpose of making mourners as distracted as any external thing can make them, it is the bitter, hopeless, unrestrained wail of this tune. There is neither peace nor resignation in it, but the very exhaustion of raving sorrow that heeds neither God nor man, but cries out, with the soulless agony of a wind-harp, its refusal to be comforted.

At length it was over, and still in that same dead calm Josephine came home to me. Mrs. Bowen was frightened, Mr. Bowen distressed. I could not think what to do, at first; but remembering how sometimes a little thing had utterly broken me down from a regained calmness after loss, some homely association, some recall of the past, I begged of Mr.

Bowen to bring up from the village Frank's knapsack, which he had found in one of his men's hands,—the poor fellow having taken care of that, while he lost his own: "For the captain's wife," he said. As soon as it came, I took from it Frank's coat, and his cap and sword. My heart was in my mouth as I entered Josephine's room, and saw the fixed quiet on her face where she sat. I walked in, however, with no delay, and laid the things down on her bed, close to where she sat. She gave one startled look at them and then at me; her face relaxed from all its quiet lines; she sank on her knees by the bedside, and, burying her head in her arms, cried, and cried, and cried, so helplessly, so utterly without restraint, that I cried, too. It was impossible for me to help it. At last the tears exhausted themselves; the dreadful sobs ceased to convulse her; all drenched and tired, she lifted her face from its rest, and held out her arms to me. I took her up, and put her to bed like a child. I hung the coat and cap and sword where she could see them. I made her take a cup of broth, and before long, with her eyes fixed on the things I had hung up, she fell asleep, and slept heavily, without waking, till the next morning.

I feared almost to enter her room when I heard her stir; I had dreaded her waking,—that terrible hour that all know who have suffered, the dim awakening shadow that darkens so swiftly to black reality; but I need not have dreaded it for her. She told me afterward that in all that sleep she never lost the knowledge of her grief; she did not come into it as a surprise. Frank had seemed to be with her, distant, sad, yet consoling; she felt that he was gone, but not utterly,—that there was drear separation and loneliness, but not forever.

When I went in, she lay there awake, looking at her trophy, as she came to call it, her eyes with all their light quenched and sodden out with crying, her face pale and unalterably sad, but natural in its sweetness and mobility. She drew me down to her and kissed me.

"May I get up?" she asked; and then, without waiting for an answer, went on,—"I have been selfish, Sue; I will try to be better now; I won't run away from my battle. Oh, how glad I am he didn't run away! It is dreadful now, dreadful! Perhaps, if I had to choose if he should have run away or—or this, I should have wanted him to run,—I'm afraid I should. But I am glad now. If God wanted him, I'm glad he went from the front ranks. Oh, those poor women whose husbands ran away, and were killed, too!"

She seemed to be so comforted by that one thought! It was a strange trait in the little creature; I could not quite fathom it.

After this, she came down-stairs and went about among us, busying herself in various little ways. She never went to the grave-yard; but whenever she was a little tired, I was sure to find her sitting in her room with her eyes on that cap and coat and sword. Letters of condolence poured in, but she would not read them or answer them, and they all fell into my hands. I could not wonder; for, of all cruel conventionalities, visits and letters of condolence seem to me the most cruel. If friends can be useful in lifting off the little painful cares that throng in the house of death till its presence is banished, let them go and do their work quietly and cheerfully; but to make a call or write a note, to measure your sorrow and express theirs, seems to me on a par with pulling a wounded man's bandage off and probing his hurt, to hear him cry out and hear yourself say how bad it must be!

Laura Lane was admitted, for Frank's sake, as she had been his closest and dearest relative. The day she came, Josey had a severe headache, and looked wretchedly. Laura was shocked, and showed it so obviously, that, if there had been any real cause for her alarm, I should have turned her out of the room without ceremony, almost before she was fairly in it. As soon as she left, Josey looked at me and smiled.

"Laura thinks I am going to die," said she; "but I'm not. If I could, I wouldn't, Sue; for poor father and mother want me, and so will the soldiers by-and-by." A weary, heart-breaking look quivered in her face as she went on, half whispering,—"But I should—I *should* like to see him!"

In September she went away. I had expected it ever since she spoke of the soldiers needing her. Mrs. Bowen went to the sea-side for her annual asthma. Mr. Bowen went with Josephine to Washington. There, by some talismanic influence, she got admission to the hospitals, though she was very pretty, and under thirty. I think perhaps her pale face and widow's dress, and her sad, quiet manner, were her secret of success. She worked here like a sprite; nothing daunted or disgusted her. She followed the army to Yorktown, and nursed on the transport-ships. One man said, I was told, that it was "jes' like havin' an apple-tree blow raound, to see that Mis' Addison; she was so kinder cheery an' pooty, an' knew sech a sight abaout nussin', it did a feller lots of good only to look at her chirpin' abaout."

Now and then she wrote to me, and almost always ended by declaring she was "quite well, and almost happy." If ever she met with one of Frank's men,—and all who were left reenlisted for the war,—he was sure to be nursed like a prince, and petted with all sorts of luxuries, and told it was for his old captain's sake. Mr. and Mrs. Bowen followed her everywhere, as near as they could get to her, and afforded unfailing supplies of such extra hospital-stores as she wanted; they lavished on her time and money and love enough to have satisfied three women, but Josey found uses for it all—for her work. Two months ago, they all came back to Dartford. A hospital had been set up there, and some one was needed to put it in operation; her experience would be doubly useful there, and it was pleasant for her to be so near Frank's home, to be among his friends and hers.

I went in, to do what I could, being stronger than usual, and found her hard at work. Her face retained its rounded outline, her lips had recovered their bloom, her curls now and then strayed from the net under which she carefully tucked them, and made her look as girlish as ever, but the girl's expression was gone; that tender, patient, resolute look was born of a woman's stern experience; and though she had laid aside her widow's-cap, because it was inconvenient, her face was so sad in its repose, so lonely and inexpectant, she scarce needed any outward symbol to proclaim her widowhood. Yet under all this new character lay still some of those childish tastes that made, as it were, the "fresh perfume" of her nature: everything that came in her way was petted; a little white kitten followed her about the wards, and ran to meet her, whenever she came in, with joyful demonstrations; a great dog waited for her at home, and escorted her to and from the hospital; and three canaries hung in her chamber;—and I confess here, what I would not to Laura, that she retains yet a strong taste for sugar-plums, gingerbread, and the "Lady's Book." She kept only so much of what Laura called her vanity as to be exquisitely neat and particular in every detail of dress; and though a black gown, and a white linen apron, collar, and cuffs do not afford much room for display, yet these were always so speckless and spotless that her whole aspect was refreshing.

Last week there was a severe operation performed in the hospital, and Josephine had to be present. She held the poor fellow's hand till he was insensible from the kindly chloroform they gave him, and, after the surgeons were through, sat by him till night, with such a calm, cheerful face, giving him wine and broth, and watching every indication of pulse or skin, till he really rallied, and is now doing well.

As I came over, the next day, I met Doctor Rivers at the door of her ward.

"Really," said he, "that little Mrs. Addison is a true heroine!"

The kitten purred about my feet, and as I smiled assent to him, I said inwardly to myself,—

"Really, she is a true woman!"

The Locket

Kate Chopin

1

ONE NIGHT IN autumn a few men were gathered about a fire on the slope of a hill. They belonged to a small detachment of Confederate forces and were awaiting orders to march. Their gray uniforms were worn beyond the point of shabbiness. One of the men was heating something in a tin cup over the embers. Two were lying at full length a little distance away, while a fourth was trying to decipher a letter and had drawn close to the light. He had unfastened his collar and a good bit of his flannel shirt front.

"What's that you got around your neck, Ned?" asked one of the men lying in the obscurity.

Ned—or Edmond—mechanically fastened another button of his shirt and did not reply. He went on reading his letter.

"Is it your sweet heart's picture?"

"'Taint no gal's picture," offered the man at the fire. He had removed his tin cup and was engaged in stirring its grimy contents with a small stick. "That's a charm; some kind of hoodoo business that one o' them priests gave him to keep him out o' trouble. I know them Cath'lics. That's how come Frenchy got permoted an never got a scratch since he's been in the ranks. Hey, French! aint I right?" Edmond looked up absently from his letter.

"What is it?" he asked.

"Aint that a charm you got round your neck?"

"It must be, Nick," returned Edmond with a smile. "I don't know how I could have gone through this year and a half without it."

The letter had made Edmond heart sick and home sick. He stretched himself on his back and looked straight up at the blinking stars. But he was not thinking of them nor of anything but a certain spring day when the bees were humming in the clematis; when a girl was saying good bye to him. He could see her as she unclasped from her neck the locket which she fastened about his own. It was an old fashioned golden locket bearing miniatures of her father and mother with their names and the date of their marriage. It was her most precious earthly possession. Edmond could feel again the folds of the girl's soft white gown, and see the droop of the angel-sleeves as she circled her fair arms about his neck. Her sweet face, appealing, pathetic, tormented by the pain of parting, appeared before him as vividly as life. He turned over, burying his face in his arm and there he lay, still and motionless.

The profound and treacherous night with its silence and semblance of peace settled upon the camp. He dreamed that the fair Octavie brought him a letter. He had no chair to offer her and was pained and embarrassed at the condition of his garments. He was ashamed of the poor food which comprised the dinner at which he begged her to join them.

He dreamt of a serpent coiling around his throat, and when he strove to grasp it the slimy thing glided away from his clutch. Then his dream was clamor.

"Git your duds! you! Frenchy!" Nick was bellowing in his face. There was what appeared to be a scramble and a rush rather than any regulated movement. The hill side was alive with clatter and motion; with sudden up-springing lights among the pines. In the east the dawn was unfolding out of the darkness. Its glimmer was yet dim in the plain below.

"What's it all about?" wondered a big black bird perched in the top of the tallest tree. He was an old solitary and a wise one, yet he was not wise enough to guess what it was all about. So all day long he kept blinking and wondering.

The noise reached far out over the plain and across the hills and awoke the little babes that were sleeping in their cradles. The smoke curled up toward the sun and shadowed the plain so that the stupid birds thought it was going to rain; but the wise one knew better.

"They are children playing a game," thought he. "I shall know more about it if I watch long enough."

At the approach of night they had all vanished away with their din and smoke. Then the old bird plumed his feathers. At last he had understood! With a flap of his great, black wings he shot downward, circling toward the plain.

A man was picking his way across the plain. He was dressed in the garb of a clergyman. His mission was to administer the consolations of religion to any of the prostrate figures in whom there might yet linger a spark of life. A Negro accompanied him, bearing a bucket of water and a flask of wine.

There were no wounded here; they had been borne away. But the retreat had been hurried and the vultures and the good Samaritans would have to look to the dead.

There was a soldier—a mere boy—lying with his face to the sky. His hands were clutching the sward on either side and his finger nails were stuffed with earth and bits of grass that he had gathered in his despairing grasp upon life. His musket was gone; he was hatless and his face and clothing were begrimed. Around his neck hung a gold chain and locket. The priest, bending over him, unclasped the chain and removed it from the dead soldier's neck. He had grown used to the terrors of war and could face them unflinchingly; but its pathos, someway, always brought the tears to his old, dim eyes.

The angelus was ringing half a mile away. The priest and the Negro knelt and murmured together the evening benediction and a prayer for the dead.

2

The peace and beauty of a spring day had descended upon the earth like a benediction. Along the leafy road which skirted a narrow, tortuous stream in central Louisiana, rumbled an old fashioned cabriolet, much the worse for hard and rough usage over country roads and lanes. The fat, black horses went in a slow, measured trot, notwithstanding constant urging on the part of the fat, black coachman. Within the vehicle were seated the fair Octavie and her old friend and neighbor, Judge Pillier, who had come to take her for a morning drive.

Octavie wore a plain black dress, severe in its simplicity. A narrow belt held it at the waist and the sleeves were gathered into close fitting wristbands. She had discarded her hoopskirt and appeared not unlike a nun. Beneath the folds of her bodice nestled the old locket. She never displayed it now. It had returned to her sanctified in her eyes; made precious as material things sometimes are by being forever identified with a significant moment of one's existence.

A hundred times she had read over the letter with which the locket had come back to her. No later than that morning she had again pored over it. As she sat beside the window, smoothing the letter out upon her knee, heavy and spiced odors stole in to her with the songs of birds and the humming of insects in the air.

She was so young and the world was so beautiful that there came over her a sense of unreality as she read again and again the priest's letter. He told of that autumn day drawing to its close, with the gold and the red fading out of the west, and the night gathering its shadows to cover the faces of the dead. Oh! She could not believe that one of those dead was her own! with visage uplifted to the gray sky in an agony of supplication. A spasm of resistance and rebellion seized and swept over her. Why was the spring here with its flowers and its seductive breath if he was dead! Why was she here! What further had she to do with life and the living!

Octavie had experienced many such moments of despair, but a blessed resignation had never failed to follow, and it fell then upon her like a mantle and enveloped her.

"I shall grow old and quiet and sad like poor Aunt Tavie," she murmured to herself as she folded the letter and replaced it in the secretary. Already she gave herself a little demure air like her Aunt Tavie. She walked with a slow glide in unconscious imitation of Mademoiselle Tavie whom some youthful affliction had robbed of earthly compensation while leaving her in possession of youth's illusions.

As she sat in the old cabriolet beside the father of her dead lover, again there came to Octavie the terrible sense of loss which had assailed her so often before. The soul of her youth clamored for its rights; for a share in the world's glory and exultation. She leaned back and drew her veil a little closer about her face. It was an old black veil of her Aunt Tavie's. A whiff of dust from the road had blown in and she wiped her cheeks and her eyes with her soft, white handkerchief, a homemade handkerchief, fabricated from one of her old fine muslin petticoats.

"Will you do me the favor, Octavie," requested the judge in the courteous tone which he never abandoned, "to remove that veil which you wear. It seems out of harmony, someway, with the beauty and promise of the day."

The young girl obediently yielded to her old companion's wish and unpinning the cumbersome, sombre drapery from her bonnet, folded it neatly and laid it upon the seat in front of her.

"Ah! that is better; far better!" he said in a tone expressing unbounded relief. "Never put it on again, dear." Octavie felt a little hurt; as if he wished to debar her from share and parcel in the burden of affliction which had been placed upon all of them. Again she drew forth the old muslin handkerchief.

They had left the big road and turned into a level plain which had formerly been an old meadow. There were clumps of thorn trees here and there, gorgeous in their spring radiance. Some cattle were gazing off in the distance in spots where the grass was tall and luscious. At the far end of the meadow was the towering lilac hedge, skirting the lane that led to Judge Pillier's house, and the scent of its heavy blossoms met them like a soft and tender embrace of welcome.

As they neared the house the old gentleman placed an arm around the girl's shoulders and turning her face up to him he said: "Do you not think that on a day like this miracles might happen? When the whole earth is vibrant with life, does it not seem to you, Octavie, that heaven might for once relent and give us back our dead?" He spoke very low, advisedly, and impressively. In his voice was an old quaver which was not habitual and there was agitation in every line of his visage. She gazed at him with eyes that were full of supplication and a certain terror of joy.

They had been driving through the lane with the towering hedge on one side and the open meadow on the other. The horses had somewhat quickened their lazy pace. As they turned into the avenue leading to the house, a whole choir of feathered songsters fluted a sudden torrent of melodious greeting from their leafy hiding places.

Octavie felt as if she had passed into a stage of existence which was like a dream, more poignant and real than life. There was the old gray house with its sloping eaves. Amid the blur of green, and dimly, she saw familiar faces and heard voices as if they came from far across the fields, and Edmond was holding her. Her dead Edmond; her living Edmond, and she felt the beating of his heart against her and the agonizing rapture of his kisses striving to awake her. It was as if the spirit of life and the awakening spring had given back the soul to her youth and bade her rejoice.

It was many hours later that Octavie drew the locket from her bosom and looked at Edmond with a questioning appeal in her glance.

"It was the night before an engagement," he said. "In the hurry of the encounter, and the retreat next day, I never missed it till the fight was over. I thought of course I had lost it in the heat of the struggle, but it was stolen."

"Stolen," she shuddered, and thought of the dead soldier with his face uplifted to the sky in an agony of supplication.

Edmond said nothing; but he thought of his messmate; the one who had lain far back in the shadow; the one who had said nothing.

Crowder's Cove: A Story of the War

Constance Fenimore Woolson

IT WAS NO shore-cove at all, but a cove in the mountains, surrounded not by water, but by the wooded sides of near peaks; there was one entrance to it, and one only—a narrow gorge opening toward the west. The spring behind the house began a little brook, which, growing into a mountain-stream, ran chattering down this gorge, where the one road made its way up painfully alongside, crossing the stony bed again and again as if seeking a better footing, but finding it not until at last it reached, breathless, the house-door. Crowder's Cove was far up in the mountains; the peaks seldom suffer level spaces so near their great chins. But this was a chance corner formed by the closely-pressed meeting sides where the great cones are crowded together near the end of their chain, that long chain which begins at Katahdin and ends at Caesar's Head, Lookout, and Kenesaw, saying, as Alabama's soft name also says, "Here we rest." It was like a little triangular shelf fitted into the corner of a room—as though some cyclop long ago had placed it there, high up under the sky, where he could keep his odds and ends conveniently. The cyclop and his odds and ends were gone, but Crowder had found the shelf, and, seeing it grassy and good for grain, he had forthwith built his house there. He was sitting now on a bench before his door, smoking a pipe.

"A pretty place; but isn't it lonely sometimes?" I said.

"It is full enough of people for me," answered John. "I don't deny that I miss Minerva, now she's gone forever; but it all came because I married Minerva. Then there was Elinor, and Sally, and my black horse Tom. Yes, it all came because I married Minerva—all."

I found out the "all" after a while—a little side-scene in the Tennessee mountains—as follows:

Miss Minerva, a middle-aged, weary teacher, had come down from her Illinois seminary for a change of air. Her health was failing, and she had laid nothing by, but sent all to her delicate fading sisters in their New Hampshire home; there was only one left now, pale little Elinor. John Crowder was a rich man, according to mountain ideas, and he was alone in the world, his wife having died some years before. He took all summer to make up his mind, and gave no sign meanwhile, but the night before Miss Minerva's departure he surprised her with a question. Miss Minerva started, trembled, and burst into tears; it was all so strange, so pitifully sad—she had not realized before that she still clung to the fancies of her youth. But the elderly lover assured her that there was no occasion for tears—he did not wish to marry her unless she were quite willing—he could look elsewhere; indeed, perhaps he had been hasty, and perhaps—And here the elderly maiden, hastily burying her fancies forever, consented. Three months afterward she had her sister Elinor resting after her long journey in the large, low south chamber up-stairs; and early in the spring, in order that John might not complain of extra expense, she took Sally Trellington as a summer boarder. Sally was a Southern girl, her good, old-fashioned name told that; Sally, Betty, Patty, and Nanny, have not lost caste so far in the cotton States. She was a big, broad-shouldered, overgrown girl, with a baby face, soft brown eyes, a fresh mouth somewhat large, and a healthy, brown-tinged skin. Her voice was charmingly rich and sweet, and all her words seemed to wear trailing skirts of velvet, they came so slowly from her careless lips, and lingered so softly on the air. (Oh, the sweet voices of the South!) The heavy coils of her hair were golden, and caught the sun-rays; all the better because two or three strands were often loose and hanging down her back. For the rest she seemed to be generally too large for her clothes, and she liked to sleep, and often did sleep twelve hours out of the twenty-four. She was an orphan, and fresh from boarding-school; her uncle had sent her up to the mountains for the summer, not well knowing what else to do with her. There was trouble in the air. "Things will be settled in the autumn," he said; "then I will have her back."

Minerva gave Sally the north chamber; there was only the narrow entry-way between the two girls, and they speedily became friends from force of propinquity, and also from the comical dissimilarity of their ideas and habits, a dissimilarity which amused the quick fancy of Elinor Kent. Sally, however, had no fancies; she did not notice that they were unlike. Near-sighted, and unobservant in mind as well as eyes, she would have walked over a cripple, begged his pardon carelessly, and then, seeing at last what she had done, she would have thrown herself down upon her knees beside him, burst into tears, and proffered all the money she had with remorseful and effusive penitence. But Elinor could have walked blindfold over a regiment of cripples without hurting one of them.

Elinor had a hundred deft little contrivances in her room to hold this and that; the very pins stood in straight rows on their cushion; she could put her hand upon any article in the dark. But Sally! One girl was rich, the other was poor; yet the rich girl's possessions looked like rags, and tatters, and beggar's gatherings, beside the neat belongings of the other. Elinor Kent was small and straight and precise; not a hair was ever displaced; her snowy little linen collar seemed a part of her. If you had come across her in the middle of the Great Desert, riding on a camel, she would have looked just the same. At least, that is what you said to your-self when you saw her. This small New England woman's spirit was at length so vexed within her by the voluminous carelessness of her new companion that she took upon herself the task of setting the strewed room in order every morning before Chloe, the small chambermaid, was let loose in the chaos, and she even began another work of supereroga-tion, repairing the rent clothes.

"Do stand still a moment, Sally," she pleaded, following, needle in hand, the flying muslin skirt whose flounces showed a long rent. And then Sally would stop good-naturedly, and stand leaning on the low fence, singing and calling to the calves, while the quick fingers made her whole again.

"I wonder why I do this," said Elinor one morning, pausing, duster in hand, before the littered bureau.

"I wonder, too," said Sally.

She was lying on the bed, caressing an absurd little flying-squirrel, too young to be anything but a ball of gray down. She had found the little wretch on the ground, where he had fallen by some mischance, and of course she must bring him home, and let him nestle in her warm hand, where he lay curled close, with one little paw holding on by her thumb, fast asleep, and seemingly well content. "Silly Bunny," said Sally, in her cooing voice, "why do you sleep all the time? Why not sit up and eat nuts?" For she had brought in a store of nuts of all kinds for her pet and left him among them in the bottom of a muff-box, a miniature Stonehenge to him, where he would inevitably have starved to death if Elinor had not come to the rescue, and unwillingly administered to the baby nutcracker warm milk on a bit of sponge.

"Of course I cannot see him starve," she said to herself, wrathfully, "but who wants him to grow? Climbing up the curtains like mad, dropping down unexpectedly on your head, creeping between the mattresses, squeezing himself under the edges of the carpets—that is what he will do! One comfort—Sally will kill him before long; she has tried him with cake, sugar, and pudding, already."

John Crowder did not ride down after the mail that month until the 20th; he brought back a letter for Sally, and a letter and papers for Elinor, besides his own sheaf of weeklies. The girls began to read at once.

"They have fired on Sumter, Minerva," said Elinor, looking up with a pale face; "now we shall have war."

"Will Prarlie has gone down to Moultrie with his company," said Sally, laughing; "I wonder how he likes it there. Lady Prarlie we used to call him."

So the news came up the mountain.

But Crowder's Cove was far away from the little post-office village, which itself also was far away from the railroad. John went on with his planting, and Minerva had lived face to face with care too long to be easily turned from her comforts by anxieties for Charleston Harbor. Sally petted the squirrel, who was growing aldermanic, and only Elinor watched the heavens. When the news came of the battle of Bull Run, she went off by herself down the gorge, and, climbing out on to a rock that overlooked the valley, she sat there for hours, thinking; her senses

75

bewildered and sore as though some one had struck her. And Northern girls all over the country were thinking in the same bewildered way; some, too, were sobbing over a telegram, or a black-edged letter.

Sally cried when she heard that her uncle had gone into the army, cried and cried until her pillow was wet; the great tears splashed through her fingers (for she could not find her handkerchief), and she was a spectacle of moist and bedraggled grief. Elinor, coming in later, found her thus, and, regarding her for the moment as the whole Southern Confederacy, began involuntarily to make ready her weapons, the great principles of that strong Northern faith of hers with which she had been holding stern vigil out on her solitary rock. But Sally did not care for principles, she only sobbed:

"Uncle has gone into the army, Elinor. Oh, I know he will be killed! I know he will be killed!"

"If he is what you say, he could not very well stay out, I suppose," began Elinor Kent, trying to put herself impartially in the uncle's place, but not succeeding very well. "With Southern principles—his State having seceded—"

But Sally did not at all appreciate the herculean effort this New England woman was making to do justice to the motives, mistaken though they might be, of the other side. She only sobbed:

"He will be killed! I know he will be killed!" And a fresh flow of tears ran down, and drabbled her limp collar anew.

"No, he won't," said Elinor, shortly, coming down from the abstract to Sally's small plane of personalities. "Take my handkerchief—do. They will make him a secretary or something of the kind; he is too old for active service while they have plenty of younger men."

"Do you think so? Do you really think so?" said Sally, eagerly.

She brightened at once; in five minutes she was playing with the squirrel, in ten her laugh rang through the house. For Master Bunny could climb a tree-branch, now, waddling a little and meeting with many narrow escapes, and all the chairs in Sally's room had branches lashed to their backs for his benefit, and were consequently, although bower-like, useless for their original purposes.

The summer wore on, and even the remote mountain-settlements began to wake. There was still a party there that called itself "neutral"; but from many a highland farm the adventurous spirits rode off down the glens by night, and in the morning they and the best horses were gone,

gone to join Zollicoffer or John Morgan. There were even a few "Union men"; but it took all their daylight to wrest a living from their stony fields, and they had no lounging-places where they could hear the news and be inspired. Each man lived with his family high up among the peaks or buried in some wild gorge, and was always at home by night-fall; for the rest, he solaced himself cannily now and then with a moder-ate drop or two of the "moonlight whisky," for which the mountains were famous, and bothered not about "the flag." John Crowder was neutral. He was neither a Northerner nor a Southerner, he said, but a mountaineer; which is like the Sunday-school boy who declared stubbornly that he was neither a Jew nor a Gentile, but a Presbyterian. Minerva felt that she could no longer deny the existence of war; but it was a far-off darkness, and meanwhile the sun shone brightly down up-on her home. If she had sold her birthright for a mess of pottage, at least the pottage was good and strong, and she was not inclined to undervalue it. Only Elinor watched; watched and waited. Think of a hot-souled, feeble-bodied girl, New England through and through, prisoned at such a time in such a place!

The first frosts came. The mortification and bewilderment of Bull Run, the indecisive mountain-fighting in West Virginia, had quenched the first eager expectation of the North, and the people began to realize that a longer and more difficult contest lay before them than they had imagined. They did not flinch, there was no flinching on either side; but they settled down to their task soberly. Sally might remain where she was, her uncle wrote, or she might spend the winter with a cousin in Alabama. Sally decided to stay where she was. Her cousin in Alabama might want her to practise, or, perhaps, to mend her clothes. She decid-ed to stay. John Crowder, still tranquilly neutral, gathered in his crops, while Minerva canned fruit. The two girls, however, were free to do as they chose, and they chose to take long walks back into Cutaway Gap. The trees on the cliffs were gorgeous with colors, the river rushed over the rocks below; at one point they could see the top of the highest mountain of the range, and they often sat on a rock out in the stream, reached by a natural bridge of stepping-stones, and gazed up at the balsam-black peak. That is, Elinor gazed. She tried to make Sally see all she saw up there; but the peak was too distant for Sally's near-sighted eyes, and she did not care about the bald stone ledges where no human foot had ever trod, and where there were gold, perhaps, and silver, and certainly rattlesnakes. In the remote, high-up glens, Elinor thought, might be the hidden stills where the moonlight whiskey was made by strange men with pistols and knives in their belts, rough-bearded fellows who rode by night to meet their customers, and required a password of them at the entrance of the cave where their contraband goods were stored. Sally listened as long as the story lasted, and then straightway forgot it all. But one evening there was something which she did not forget. The girls had loitered late on their rock; suddenly they heard the sound of hoofs coming up the cañon; they had never heard anything there before but the birds and the water.

"Sit close," whispered Elinor; "you are so big, Sally. Put your head down; the trees on the bank will hide us, I think."

She was startled; there were no farms in that direction, and no one rode through dark, wild Cutaway Gap for pleasure. They waited; this is what they saw: a man rode by on horseback, supporting a boy wounded and bleeding; the stripling's pale face hung over toward the girls as the strong steed galloped by, into their sight and out again; then there was only the sound of the hoofs, which grew fainter and fainter, until there was nothing but the old rush of the river.

"How could they shoot him?" said Sally, tremulously—"how could they? Poor boy!"

"Guerrillas, I suppose," answered her companion. "We shall not see armies marching through these mountains, probably, but guerrillas will be shooting each other back and forth from behind these trees and over the tops of these rocks before long."

"Not here?" said Sally, looking fearfully around.

"Why not here as well as anywhere? Isn't there war in the land, child?"

"I never thought it would come *here*," said big, soft-hearted Sally, keeping close hold of her companion's arm as they hastened back to the cove. When they reached the house, Elinor told what they had seen, simply and without comment. John Crowder muttered something about fighting people being all "a pack of fools," but Minerva followed her sister out into the dark doorway.

"Did you notice whether they were our men?" she asked, in a whisper.

"They were not in uniform; of course I could not tell," said Elinor. "But, oh, sister, how wrong it seems for us to be here!"

"I don't know about that," responded Minerva, sharply, veering around instinctively to the defense of her pottage. "If we were at the North we should have to work for our living, and I know what that is. You have but little bodily strength, Elinor, and even mine has broken down; we could do nothing. Besides, there is no harm in our being here; we are neutral."

"Neutral!" echoed the other, with bitter scorn. Then, remembering the elder sister's long toil and pains, she stopped. "Forgive me, Minerva," she said; "I forget sometimes all you have done for me." But her heart was hot within her all the same. When she went to her room that night, she paused a moment at Sally's open door. The girl was asleep, with a smile on her face; and the broad white shoulders, the large, round curves and outlines under the tossed draperies of the bed, and the flushed, soft cheeks, were alike distasteful to her. She could not have told why; but she closed her door irritably, and said to herself, "I am glad I am not a great ox-like thing like that!"

Winter came, and lethargy. There was little suffering in the West during the winter of '61; war was new, and supplies plenty. The South would have liked better guns for her armies and the North better generals for hers; but they shifted and changed about what they had, and drilled bravely. John Crowder was holding his grain for higher prices; his barns were full, and he foresaw a rise. Not much snow fell at the cove; the wind howled down the gorges, and the roads were now frozen in long ruts, now thawed to deep-red mire; this is the Southern mountain winter. Elinor found no great deeds to do in all those long months, despite her great longing, and by January she had worked herself up to such a pitch that she began to plan how she could flee northward through the lines and reach the Ohio River. Minerva would never consent; so Minerva should know nothing about it. But the younger sister studied county maps, asked a quiet question now and then, reckoned over her store of money, and planned to increase it. Minerva had none, she knew; Sally had it, and would have given it freely, unquestioning, but she would not ask it. It seemed to her too much like the spoiling of the Egyptians, which transaction she had never, even in childhood, approved. She took two of a neighbor's girls to teach, and she did plain sewing for the few who wanted it.

"If it amuses you, Elinor, I will not object," said Mrs. Crowder; "but I never intended that you should work here."

"It does amuse me," replied Elinor.

In this manner she trenched and dug her way along toward her object, silently, patient as an ant, and steady as a machine; gaining only an inch or two a day, perhaps, as when she took two weeks to persuade John Crowder that he wanted another horse, and that the blacksmith's white mare down in the village was the one he wanted. She was no horsewoman; in fact, she was afraid of a horse; but she thought she might ride gentle Bess when the time came, the time that should see her doing those great deeds, crossing the lines to her own country and helping on the cause. How she should help she did not know, but she was sure there would be something for her ardent hands to do. "I will try the hospital," she said to herself; "I should like that best."

Suddenly came a stroke that crushed her plans; a fever struck her and laid her helpless upon her bed.

"You have not taken your usual care of yourself, Elinor; you seem to have forgotten lately how little strength you have. I never intended that you should work here," said anxious Minerva.

"Intended! intended! And can *I* have no intentions," thought the younger sister, feverishly.

Sally was forbidden the room. Her overflowing affection and awkwardness, her flying skirts and inconvenient kisses, distracted the poor patient and drove her half wild. "I cannot stand her knocking the chairs about any longer," she declared.

So Minerva gently forbade her entrance, and Sally, retreating to her own room, confided to her pillow that she was a miserable, unhappy girl, that nobody loved her, and that she thought she would like to die and be buried somewhere under a willow. After a while, however, she perceived the spicy odor of gingerbread which Dinah was baking in the kitchen, and concluded to go down and get some. Then the dogs must be fed, and the bird wanted water; and there was Bunny climbing up the curtain, and positively gnawing a hole in it! She forgot all about her griefs, and the sick-room was left in peace. "She is a whirlwind of a girl," said Minerva.

Spring came. The mountains were the same; their evergreen brightens not, neither does it fade; but along the brooks and through the gorges the nut-trees and the oaks put on their fresh foliage, and the early flowers came out. People riding through the lowlands on the east and on the west began to think again of the pink-marble ledges, the gold, the silver, and the iron hidden far within the dark range; but war was in the land, and they said "not yet." Like enchanted princesses the gleaming metals still wait within. "Will the prince never come," they say, "the beautiful, bright Prince of Steam?"

Elinor sat by the window and gazed off down the gorge into the budding lowlands. She was well again, but pale and worn, for she had never once stopped brooding—brooding, well or ill, upon the one subject that filled her heart: "Oh, to do something! to do something for the cause!"

Sally, sitting on the floor by her side, sang "Bonnie Dundee."

"He spurred to the foot of the high castle-rock,
And to the dark Gordon he gallantly spoke,
'Your grace in short space shall have tidings of me,
Or low lies the bonnet of Bonnie Dundee!
There are hills beyond Pentland, and streams beyond Forth,
If there's lords in the Southland there's chiefs in the North,
There are wild dunnie-wassals three thousand times three,
Will cry "hey for the bonnet of Bonnie Dundee"'!"

sang Sally in her rich voice.

"You do not care much about it though, do you?" said Elinor, slowly.

"'Bonnie Dundee'?"

"Yes; that is the spirit of it, the defiance and undying determination. Sally, did you care about Donelson?"

For a wave of rage, grief, and surprise, had swept over the entire South when word came that Fort Donelson had fallen.

"Donelson?" said Sally—"Donelson? Oh, yes, I remember now—up on the Cumberland River. But uncle was not there, nor any one I know, Elinor; they are all either in Richmond or Charleston."

"I mean the surrender—in fact, the war as a whole, child. Do you care about it?"

"Of course I do," said Sally, flushing a little. "But you know we are so far away, Elinor, so far away from everything."

"We *are* far away," brooded the Northern girl, gazing off into the blue distant lowlands. "The war is down there. Oh, how I wish, how I wish I could go!"

But, not long after that, the war accommodatingly came up; came up at last to Crowder's Cove.

It was only a fringe of the mantle, a breath of the whirlwind, an edge of the storm; but to John Crowder it was like the judgment-day. Indeed, it was worse, for John had never harbored much fear of the judgment; was he not a solid, respectable farmer? and could any one say aught against him? Nay, would it not be well if others followed his example, especially in the matter of fences and drains?

"Turn out, old man, and give us some horse-feed," called a voice one night, while impatient hands rapped at the doors and windows. "Ah, you are there, are you? Whom are you for?"

John, candle in hand, replied that he was for nobody; he was neutral.

"So much the worse for you, I reckon," said the boy-officer in charge of the party; "small respect have we for neutrals. If you had come boldly out now, and said 'Union,' we should have admired your pluck, and we might even have given you something for your feed. But, as it is—neutral! Bah! Confound all neutrals, say I.—Go on, men."

The men went on; feed for a hundred horses was soon *en route* down the glen.

The moon was shining, and the three women, gazing from the darkened upper window, noted gray uniforms.

"*Your* soldiers," said Elinor, scornfully, when Minerva had gone down to comfort her spouse, who was loudly lamenting.

"Mine?" said Sally. "Why, I never saw the men in my life before."

"You are the best girl in the world, Sally. But I wish, I do wish, you were—"

"What?"

"A foeman worthy of my steel," said Elinor, drumming impatiently on the window-pane. "Go to bed, you great, sleepy creature; do."

"I know I am big, and I know I am apt to be sleepy," said Sally, deprecatingly; "but I cannot help it, Elinor; and I think it is unkind of you to mention it so often."

"So it is; I beg your pardon."

Sally went back to bed, and was asleep in five minutes; but Elinor sat long by the window, her eyes fixed thoughtfully on the open granary-door, its broken lock and hinges shining in the moonlight.

A week later there was an untimely spring-storm; the wind stripped the tender young leaves from the trees, and the rain washed out the newly-planted seeds. In the middle of the storm, in the middle of the night, there came another rapping on John Crowder's door.

"Come out, old man; we've got to levy on your live-stock here. Whom are you for?"

"Say 'Union' this time," whispered Minerva.

"I won't," said John, hastily dressing himself.

He opened the door, and the men tramped in, and filled the house; they were wet and weary, and again demanded whom he was for.

"For nobody," said stubborn John; "I am a neutral."

"Oh, that's the story, is it? I have heard that tale before," said the sergeant in command, sarcastically. "Neutral! Why don't you tell the truth, and come plank out with 'Confederate'? You'd have a better chance, I guess, old chap. Neutral, indeed! I'd be one side or the other, and not on the fence, if I were you.—Go ahead, boys. Find the pitch-pine and light up; give yer half an hour for the job."

The gazing women above saw the lights flashing in the rain while the men went to and fro, driving out the animals and collecting them together, loading their horses meanwhile with as much forage as they could carry. Owing to Elinor's illness, the two saddle-horses, Black Tom and the mare, had been removed to a distant shed behind a clump of trees, that they might not disturb her at night with the sound of their hoofs on the floor of their stalls. This saved them; but everything else that went on four feet was driven off down the gorge before John Crowder's very eyes, and the cove was left desolate.

"O sister, they were our men this time!" whispered Elinor, nervously.

"I do not care whose they are, but one thing I do know—they are thieves," said the weeping housewife.

As for Sally, she had not noticed the uniforms at all; she had staid up-stairs with all the doors locked, and peeped through the blinds, trembling.

John Crowder was furiously angry.

"I've paid dollar for dollar all my life, and now I am robbed, openly robbed, and by men in uniform, too! I'll have the law on 'em, you see!" he said.

He saddled Black Tom and rode down to the village, only to find it half in ashes, and the people sullen, with few words to give him, and little sympathy for his loss.

"You haven't had your house burned over your head, have you?" said one.

"Have you lost two sons killed in battle?" demanded a gray-haired man, sternly. "If not, hold your peace."

But John would not hold his peace. At last he found a lawyer; lawyers are obliged to be sympathetic.

"I want the law on 'em," said John.

The lawyer began to prepare "a statement of grievances."

"Feed for one hundred horses, and all your live-stock stolen, as I understand, feloniously and violently appropriated, by Federal soldiers last night—"

"No; the feed was another time," said John. "They took that a week ago."

"Ah! the same parties, I suppose? Feloniously and violently appropriated, by Federal soldiers—"

"No; the first were Confederates, I tell yer."

"A totally different matter," said the lawyer, throwing down his pen, irritably. "I am surprised that you should complain of such a simple business transaction, sir. If they took the feed, they needed it for military purposes, of course, and you will be paid by applying at department headquarters. You told them who you were, I presume, and they gave you a signed receipt?"

"I told them I was a neutral, and they gave me nothing but sass," said John.

"Neutral! But I might have known it; those mountains are full of the cowardly rascals!" said the lawyer to himself. He was a partially crippled man, and could not go to the war, or he would never have been there at his desk. But he said to himself wrathfully, "Neutral, is he! I'll fix him!" And then he "regretted" that it would be impossible for him to appear in this business, and ordered "the gentleman's horse." There was not another lawyer in the village.

John Crowder rode angrily back up the mountain, nor would he speak a word for two days. Then he began to prepare a statement of grievances on his own account, and in his own cramped handwriting, following the shape of each letter with his tongue, and bending doggedly over his work as the hours came round when he had been accustomed to feed his animals, and reminded him of his loss. His wife, however, wept openly whenever she looked at the empty pens and stalls.

"Minerva, *do* you know where you are?" demanded Elinor.

"Only too well," sighed Mrs. Crowder; "that was Brown Jenny's stall."

"I mean politically, sister. Do you know whether you are a Northerner or a Southerner?"

"The cows had no politics, at any rate," said Mrs. Crowder, with tears.

It never rains but it pours. A few days afterward a party of bushwhackers, disguised and masked, came trooping into the cove at dawn, and burned all John Crowder's full barns.

"Hey, old John," they said, dancing and jumping around him in their fantastic garb, and bellowing in his ears, "it isn't good for you to have so much grain, John; it makes you proud, John, and pride is a sin."

"Are you Confederates or Union men this time?" roared John, his heavy face purple with rage.

"Why, we're neither, brother; we're neutrals like yourself, to be sure!"

But the lawyer down in the village could have told a different story.

Before that day was done, or the smoking barns had grown cold, they heard horses again coming up the gorge.

"There is nothing now for 'em to take, unless they take ourselves," said John, grimly.

The visitors, however, did not wish to take this time, but to leave, and what they wanted to leave was a wounded man, a youth, who rode his horse with difficulty, one foot hanging helpless, swathed in bandages.

"It is that same boy!" said Sally, starting back from the window.

"I would like to leave this young man here for a while," began one of the strangers; "he is badly but not dangerously hurt, and only needs rest and attention. He will pay you for your trouble. May I ask, sir, how this happened?" he added, glancing at the burned barns and the desolation around him.

"You may," said John.

"How, then?"

"Raskills!"

"Federals or Confederates?"

"Both."

"And you?"

"I am a neutral," said John.

"I believe he would maintain that at the stake," thought Minerva, anxiously listening.

"Bah!" said the stranger, "I haven't much confidence in neutrals. Isn't there anybody here with decided opinions of some kind? I would rather trust my nephew to an out-and-out Yankee than to a neutral—so called."

"I am an out-and-out Yankee," said Elinor, appearing at the head of the stairs; but a flying figure passed her.

"And *I* am a Southerner," said Sally, rushing breathlessly out to the stranger's side. "Never fear, sir. I will take care of your nephew my own self, my very own self."

He looked down into her eager eyes and smiled.

"I should know you for a Southerner anywhere," he said.

"Of course you would. I—but look! he is fainting!" She sprang to the side of the other horse; the poor lad swayed, and fell heavily over into her arms.

"I am glad I am big," thought Sally, exultingly, standing firm with her burden, while the elder man dismounted to come to her assistance. Cameron Halisey was carried into Minerva's spare room, and there the three women tended him. Elinor was the best nurse, but his eyes followed Sally; her Southern accent fell sweetly upon his homesick ears, and her careless ways suited him better than Elinor's strict little rules. It was to Sally he talked, and, as strength came slowly back, the two would sit together at the edge of the gorge for hours. The boy had lost a brother and two cousins in battle, for they had all gone into the army together, clan-fashion; they had died ghastly deaths, and he had seen them die, so perhaps it was natural that he should turn from Northern Elinor, and find comfort in pouring his hopes, his plans, and his ardor into the Southern girl's willing ears. Sally learned much during those days. They talked, and talked, and talked. Elinor often wondered what they could be talking about; *she* had never found Sally either able or willing to hold her own in any long conversation.

At length the time came for Halisey to go; he had received word of some movement, and was on fire to be off. He whistled and sang as he put his arms in order, and twenty times a day he went down the gorge, and waited at the foot of the sentinel-rock, as if expecting some one. His horse was in fine condition, and Minerva had mended his little stock of worn clothes, and furtively added a few articles. "He is a mere boy—not more than eighteen," she said, as if half in defense of her kind deeds. "Why will they let such children go into their army?"

"He can shoot, even if he is a mere boy," replied Elinor, sharply; and then, having asserted her principles, she, too, went off and put something secretly into the little bundle.

One bright morning, soon after this, away galloped young Halisey; no messenger had come, but he would not wait any longer. Sally came back from the gorge, whither she had gone to see him off, with sparkling eyes. "Isn't he brave?" she said. "Twice wounded—for it was he we saw over there in the gap, and now this second time—yet off he goes to join—oh, I forgot. Where is Bunny? It is so long since I have played with Bunny."

Elinor looked after her for a moment, then she dismissed the subject from her mind. "She never means anything," she thought.

That night, while they sat at the supper-table, a face appeared at the open door. "Lieutenant Halisey is here, I believe? What! not in? And I haven't a moment to wait! How provoking! But just tell him, will you, that the Feds will be at Exton some time to-night, or at dawn, and our boys, coming across from the west, are going to pounce down upon them, and bag them all. General B—— is with them, badly wounded; they are tired and fagged, and we shall have an easy catch. They are coming by way of the north road, and will probably camp on Exton Hill; Halisey will understand. Just tell him, please."

He was off again; only a foolish, hot-headed Alabama boy like Halisey himself. An older campaigner would not have called through an open door in that way, and an older campaigner would infallibly have waited for supper, if there was any to be had. But in those early days, before hardship had descended upon the land, the hot-headed Southern boys did not wait for supper.

The party at the table sat silently gazing into each other's faces until the last echo of the horse's hoofs had died away. Then John Crowder delivered his usual remark about "fools," finding solace, apparently, in calling even a solitary specimen like that "a pack," and, rising, left the room.

"Oh, dear, I hope nobody will be hurt," said Minerva, nervously looking into the teapot.

"Cameron will get there in time!" cried Sally, springing up triumphantly, unable to keep silence longer; "that is where he has gone. He would not wait any longer for the message; he knew they were coming across country, and he was determined to be in the next skirmish. Good luck to him!"

Elinor sat quietly in her place, with her eyes down; her face had grown slightly paler, and she clasped her hands tightly together under the table. Here was her chance! After long waiting Fate had smiled at last. Exton was only twelve miles away; the tired Federal soldiers were marching thither by the north road; and Bess was in the stable! As soon as she could command her voice and limbs, she rose and went to her own room, pleading a headache. Sally came to her door, as usual, on her way to bed; but the other, busy with her preparations, only called out her good-night greetings, and did not show herself. "She would never suspect anything," she thought; "still I *do* look pale, and she would be wanting to do all sorts of things for me, as usual. I cannot let her in."

When the house was quiet, she stole out, clad in a plain, dark water-proof dress, a black straw-hat tied firmly down with a cord. Lifting a window softly, she crept out on to the piazza and made her way through the moonlight and shadows down to the stable. The side-saddle, which had belonged to Crowder's first wife, hung on the wall; with trembling hands she saddled Bess, and led the gentle creature out on to the grass. Black Tom, the strong, vicious beast, a terror to all the three women, eyed her knowingly, while she labored with the straps, as much as to say, "Oho, young woman, is *that* your game?" She led Bess across the grassy slope of the cove, through the fields and down the gorge, and then, at the foot of the sentinel-rock, she mounted with the aid of a stump and rode away.

It was midnight. The valley lay swathed in silver mist below her, and the peaks round about looked softer and more kind than usual in the still moonlight. She knew the road, and Bess was fleet and gentle; yet her old hands trembled on the bridle, and she looked back over her shoulder at every step. Behind the trees she knew so well, forms seemed to be lurking, and faces were peering from the corners of the friendly old fences. Is there any beginning or end to the physical cowardice of a woman? Yet sometimes she is great through her very fears. For a man does a bold deed, and is not afraid; a woman does it, and is afraid—yes, even unto death. Which shows the most courage?

After a while a strange thing happened. Intuitive perception and deliberate purpose came into collision and tried their lances against each other's shields. Sally Trellington came into view, riding Black Tom, and bound on the same errand as herself! O woman, didst try to outwit a woman?

Down the glen, over the bridge, and round the curve, galloped Sally, holding on with one hand, and with the other plying the whip, while Tom, the vicious, the terrible beast, with his head stretched forward and ears laid back, dashed madly by. Sally had only a man's saddle upon which she rode woman-fashion, reckless of her unsteady seat; she seemed to cling and grow to the horse with every muscle in her body, with her whole frame.

"Aha!" she cried, "you thought to deceive me, Elinor Kent. But *I* suspected—*I* was watching; and I'll be there before you!"

She had jumped on the horse just as she was, in her white dress; she wore no hat, and her loosened golden hair streamed behind her as she flew by; there was even a rose in the falling braids, gathered and placed there carelessly in the morning. In an instant the other girl's fears vanished; her cheeks burned hotly, she put Bess to her full speed, and galloped after the powerful black, whose hoofs were now thundering down the road ahead. The blood tingled to the ends of her fingers; to be baffled by Sally! Had she not thought and planned for months? Sally had never planned at all. Had she not purpose, principle? Sally had neither. The very horse she was riding had been purchased at her own instigation months before, while Sally was eating red apples and paying with Bunny! She put the whip to Bess, and thought with anguish that, although she was fleet, Tom was strong, and in the long miles his strength would tell. On they flew, now near together, now far apart, now within speaking distance, now out of sight of each other; but the black horse kept the lead. It was a terrible pace to hold down the mountain, where the road was steep and rocky; but they never faltered. They dashed across the brooks and up the ascents, they galloped down the glens and through the gorges, and miles soon lay between them and the quiet cove where they had been girls together and friends.

"Never more friends!" thought Elinor fiercely, clinching her hands and her teeth. But Sally did not think at all even or clinch; she only rode.

They were down the mountain at last—a level piece of road lay before them. The horses had fallen into a regular gallop—the black still in front, but not so far that Elinor could not hear every now and then the gay laugh of the Southern girl borne back on the wind. It was very hard for Elinor; but she had recovered her senses now, and, sitting her horse squarely, she calculated her chances. Tom was strong; but Tom was also vicious. If he should show his temper now!

He did.

When they came to the little river which they must ford, Tom decided to rest awhile with his legs in the water, and take a good, long, slow drink. In vain Sally coaxed him, in vain she urged; there he stood with his head down, drinking and switching his sides with his long tail; while Bess, thirsting, too, but docile, darted by and took the lead. As Elinor passed, Sally, in her wrath and disappointment, burst out crying—crying aloud with great sobs like a child.

"Go back, Sally," called Elinor, over her shoulder; and she said it not unkindly.

"Never!" cried Sally, brokenly, yet with defiance in her voice; "and I'll pass you yet, Elinor Kent!"

"Now, Bess, do your utmost," said Elinor.

The mare did her utmost—she flew down the valley like a bird; Elinor's heart was beating fast, she had won the race after all. Dear old Tom! Dear, obstinate old Tom! Dear, delightful, vicious old Tom!

But Tom had his little ways. When he had finished drinking and switching his legs with his tail, off he started again, and, biding his time, with a long, low stretching pace, he came cantering down the valley like a horse going by steam; you could have beaten time for an orchestra by the regular sound of his hoofs. Elinor saw him coming, or rather she heard him, for she would not look back. She threw off her shawl to lighten the load, and gave Bess the rein. They passed through the sleeping post-village like a flash; they crossed the long covered bridge in the echoing darkness, and were out again on the moonlit road; they could see Exton now. Black Tom was close behind, but he was a wise horse, and did not hurry his gait; he knew his speed. More miles were passed, and he was gaining, gaining. Up he came slowly, now his nose, now his shoulders, now his fore-feet, in sight of Elinor's back-glancing eyes; then he stretched himself forward a little as though on the whole he thought he would, and his black head came up even with the mare's quivering nostrils.

The two horses galloped abreast.

How the two riders looked at each other! You would not have known them for girls. With parted lips, set teeth, and pallid faces, they were like avenging Fates. Only their eyes, flashing fire, showed the burning life within. They could not speak. They hardly breathed.

Inch by inch, inch by inch, the black horse gained; until he gradually drew his whole length ahead, and took the lead. Sally, in her joy, bent and kissed his flowing mane more than once.

Poor Bess had done her utmost; but she was a slender little creature, and had seen her best days. Black Tom had muscles of steel.

The clouds, which had been gathering, now partially obscured the moon; they were nearing the cross-roads. Bess still kept close behind; Elinor calculated. Had the Federals reached Exton? Should she gallop straight to the hill or out the north road to meet them? Sally, of course, would turn off to the west. Elinor hesitated a second; then took the north road. It was dark now, and the wind had risen, a storm was coming. She turned her head where a level space between two ridges gave her a view of the town, and behold! camp-fires on the hill beyond. They were there, then; and she had lost five minutes. O rage! In a breath she had turned Bess, and was dashing down the bed of a brook across the fields straight toward the hill; there was an old track there, she knew, and Bess must follow it somehow; she gave her the rein, nor tried to guide her. She *must* save time now; every second counted. "Fly, Bess! good Bess, fly!"

The little band of Federal soldiers, weary and worn, were resting on the hill till dawn; the wounded officer with them was under shelter, waiting for a taste of the coffee over the fire. One comfort—there was no enemy this side of the river; they were safe enough, they thought, except from the rain-storm coming up from the west. But there was something else coming up from the west. They had not counted upon the lightning movements of Morgan's men, who, crossing the country toward Chattanooga, had heard of this little covey of game, and had turned aside to bag it. They were coming along that way when the apparition of Sally in her white dress, mounted on Black Tom, her cheeks scarlet, her eyes blazing, and her golden hair streaming over her shoulders, quickened their pace. She told her story, panting.

"Oh, hurry!" she cried; "get there before her—do! do!"

And they hurried. Their Kentucky horses knew how to hurry; they had not eaten blue grass for nothing.

Sally rode with Cameron Halisey. All she said was "hurry!" He hardly knew her for the same girl. She had burst into full bloom in a night.

And the tired Federals saw a vision also. A white horse galloped into their midst, and the rider, a small, pale-faced woman, cried:

"To arms! They are coming! They are coming!"

But she was just too late; they had already come. The Federals found themselves surrounded, and the bravest of them could only surrender.

At her own request Elinor Kent was sent northward through the lines. "I have long wished to go," was all she said. Sally came and threw her arms around her, and cried, and begged her forgiveness again and again. But Elinor did not speak; she could not.

Oh! Sally was the pride, and the belle, and the glory of Morgan's men that night. Exton woke up and found itself in the hands of friends. Exton did not always know its friends from its foes, but these were gay boys, at any rate, and they held high festival there until noon the next day. Then they rode off toward Chattanooga, sending Sally southward to her Alabama cousin, under the charge of an officer's wife, with a special guard of honor.

And in the Northern papers a few days afterward occurred this item: "Morgan's cavalry surprised and captured two companies of infantry out on scouting duty last week, in Karne County, Tennessee. Among the prisoners was General Blank." That was all.

Elinor Kent served in the hospitals all through the war. Some time afterward she heard of Sally.

"She is married, you know," said her informant.

"To Cameron Halisey?"

"Oh, no; he was only a boy. Her husband is a man of note down there, and Sally is one of the handsomest women I ever saw."

"Rather large, isn't she?"

"Large? Why, she is a Venus of Milo, madam, a real Venus of Milo! Is it possible you did not think her beautiful?" said the informant, thinking to himself how blind this plain little woman must be! Blind? Jealous, perhaps.

"She was very young when I knew her," said Miss Kent, turning away.

Turkey Hunt

Alberta Pierson Hannum

FOR THE FULL time of year, things were looking lean. The cornfield was nothing but a slantwise piece of ground torn up by its roots, with here and there a stalk lying dry and tramped on by soldier shoes. The open log barn cried alike for plundered horse and hay, the woods standing close by the back fence seemed not so friendly now with the cowbells silent in it. The unpainted slab house looked starved; perhaps the few hens scratching, more from habit than hope, in the barren yard, made it seem so. A lone pig rooted near the doorstep.

"Hit's got to live till butcherin' time," said the woman in the house, looking out at it. "Hit's our meat for the rest of the winter."

"Don't you go to be troubled, Clarinda. This war'll be over by winter, then I'll be home to stay, and fill that old smoke house full to bustin' with wild meat—and hit's better'n hog meat any day."

"Oh, Davy!" The woman, who was not very old, seventeen—and looking not a day over—turned away from the sorry outdoors toward her husband, and was heartened. He was in Lee's gray, to be sure, but he was here: hers for a day and a night, anyway.

"Oh, Davy, hit's so good to have you. I wish you never would go back to that old war."

"Sh—what a thing to say! They *need* me down yander."

She had a quick and unworthy thought, this girl wife did, that she and the babe needed him too. And with the thought came back that sucked dry feeling around her heart which had so much been there since he had gone off warring. But she hid her fears under a little prayer and said: "Shore, that's what I know. We'll kill us a chicken and have dumplin's you can think about till you git home ag'in."

"Dumplin's?"

She nodded triumphantly. "I got a smidgen of flour hid away under the bed tick."

And they were very gay while she wrung a scrawny fowl's neck and plucked its feathers off. David plagued and deviled her and took on generally till she declared they wouldn't be worth shucks, neither chicken nor dumplings! Contentedly the while, Matt, the baby, pushed a low stool back and forth across the floor. Once, after sober consideration, he backed up to it and sat down—smack—missing it entirely, his legs spread wide, and his eyes. How they laughed! With Davy catching the surprised little fellow up in his arms and hugging him.

An hour later found him still holding the child, jigging it up and down on his knee, with the sun full on them both, and David knowing to his bones the content of an August noon in the mountains, clear and hot and good to feel.

"Now," said Clarinda. The chicken he had been smelling for an hour was piled brown and brave on a platter, and the dumplings were floating in the best bowl.

Over the baby's rumpled towhead their eyes met in full appreciation of the feast: the riotous gaiety that goes with deliberate improvidence, the full consciousness of a security that cannot last, and that sudden sucked dry feeling in both their breasts. The baby wriggled down from his father's loosened hold and made a gleeful lurch toward the table. But before he ever reached it, before either of them could dart to haul him back, a sound broke up the whole plan of the feast. The dull, even sound of men marching down a dirt road.

Clarinda stood paralyzed, remembering whispered outrages in other neighborhoods at the hands of Kirk's marauders. David slid to a shadow by the door where he could look down the road and see dust rising about as high as the berry bushes alongside, and men in blue above it.

Just a hantel of them—rag-tag and bobtail, for the war had been going on two years now. They might be furriners, or they might be neighbors (mountain men were divided in their sympathy), but whichever they were, they were Federals.

With a step backward, keeping his eye all the while on the road coming toward the house, he felt for the laurel hooks on the wall where his gun rested.

"Davy!" It was protest against all violence; it was fear; it was indignation at this interruption of their time together. "Hide in the loft." At the same time, with presence of mind, she grabbed up a chicken that was just stepping over the threshold. It squawked in fright as she flung up the lid of a chest by the fireplace and dropped it in. "That's one chicken they won't git," grimly. She gave up, as lost, another which had evaded her clutch and now was flying and running distractedly in front of the advancing terror, its wings flapping. Then, imploringly, "Davy!" as he continued to stand illy concealed in the door shadow.

The first of the straggling file of blue was even with the furthest corner of the yard by now. For an instant David experienced the same sensation that he might have in a smoke-filled woods while he waited behind a tree for some instinct of war to guide him in his next move. But that deadly casualness did not last the instant out. For the baby, catching sight of strange men, flung both his arms about his father's legs and clung to him for dear life. David looked down. He saw the little tad venture to show his face for another peek at the moving, looming awfulness out front, then wriggle back to safety. Davy felt him, close and depending. He dropped his hand to the flaxen head. A second chicken with beady, scared eyes and a red comb was being dropped by Clarinda's resolute hands into the chest.

"Take away my plate, and you and the youngin eat." He swung up the ladder into the loft.

Even though the soldiers could turn in any place now—for the fence out front was broken and scattered—she took time to go with him, with her eyes, into his hiding. Then, her young mouth old, she hurried the platter of chicken and all but a small dish of dumplings into the cupboard. Mechanically she sat shoveling dough bits into the youngin's mouth while he lolled against her, pushing the table edge luxuriantly with bare toes. His gaze upon her was contented; the strange men were forgotten.

Up in the loft David lay on the floor, propped up by one elbow, peering out through a crack in the logs. He did not recognize any of the intruders, so calculated they were furriners. Beside him was his gun, ready to pick up and aim down the loft hole if they showed any meanness when they came in.

But he heard an order cracked out. The marching column double-quicked on past the house, with the pig ambling out to see why, and the midday sun hurrying to hit the muzzles of briskened arms. David was surprised. Evidently this was not just a foraging party—perhaps they had been cut off from their company. Nevertheless they appeared, through the dust they were raising, ready to drop and hungry. Not nearly so hungry as all of Lee's men looked, however.

Had this observation occurred to him at any other time except now—under fire, in camp, retreating, advancing—it would have stuck in his gizzard. But the feel of his least one was still warm with him, and the fellowiness of the last hour with his wife-woman had made fighting for some far away and absent cause not worth more than a slight rise of emotion which dropped again quickly. Abstractedly then, he followed the enemy by with no especial ill-will.

Until one, with his blue coat open and his whitish shirt showing, reached out and with a deft sideswiping of hand and foot pulled the pig into the middle of the column. There was the sound of muffled laughter and pig squeals. The rear guard marched close and irregularly down the road, with the meat that was to have lasted Davy's homefolks all winter marching with it.

Through the crack the glint of sun on muzzle made a blazing smear in front of the watcher's eyes.

From below came a quick scraping of chair and cautious: "Davy, they're gone. But better you stay up thar apiece—I'll keep the chicken hotted."

There was no answer. A moment earlier David had risen, on high toes had stepped across to the low window hole, and dropped with his gun to the ground.

Stealing from house to barn to cedar to fence corner, he made the woods in safety. Keeping in its shelter, he skirted the upper side of the looted cornfield, then dropped abruptly with it and the road and the blue men marching, to a cloistered level spot. Looking back, he could not now see the chimney of his house, although he was not many yards away.

Here the company halted. Immediately that the word was given, there was a willing scramble for firewood and a good deal of scuffing over who would stick the hog. One big soldier good-humoredly pawed the others off, grabbed the squealing animal, and straddled it, while another, with his sleeves up and his knife out, cleared himself a working space and deftly jabbed into the middle of a grunt.

Taking quick stock of the trees about him, David chose a tall sycamore with a magnificent spread. He was up in it in a minute. Now he could see his chimney smoke, his whole house and yard sitting bare in the sun. Looking the other way he could see the barbecue blaze shimmering in the noon heat. The man with his sleeves rolled up now had his right arm up to the elbow inside the male brute's belly-slit. From his place of vantage David looked on. That was a job of work for Clarinda this winter when he was far away and the weather bitter and food for the youngin scarce. She would not pull and yank like that, but stick her brown arm in and work and loosen carefully. He did not reflect further. A single word was in his mind. War. Without any excitation of feeling, he gave a wild turkey call.

Two of the men lying on their backs at a distance from the butchering scene raised their heads and listened. After a time, David repeated it. A third soldier on yon side the fire wheeled around. "Turkey! Boys, it's a feast!" He picked up his gun and made for the woods, with laughter and advice thrown after him.

Up in the sycamore the Confederate smiled and, with his own weapon leveled, watched the eagerness yet prudence of the other's approach. To guide him came softly again the wild game cry. It was not a big woods, nor uncommon deep, and so, sun-speckled. From sun to shadow, sun to shadow, the man in blue came on, and when he got near enough for David to see that he was a pleasant enough old fellow with food in his beard, he fired. The Yankee dropped with a bullet hole in his chest and his gun teetering across his body. He lay groaning. Davy turned his face homeward. There in the yard was Clarinda looking distractedly for him. Again sounded the turkey call, this time as if from a greater distance.

The two men flat on their backs down in the camp raised up as before and one of them got on his feet.

"Old Jo must have missed. Guess I'll have to go bring down that gobbler myself."

The pig now was swung up on an improvised spit over the fire, and there was even more joshing this hunter than there had been the first. The Federal army's heart was growing bigger, as its nostrils filled with wood smoke and the first smacking of hog juice on the flame.

When the second man, turkey-hunting and looking up, came into David's particular patch of sun, he almost stumbled over the writhing body of the comrade. But before he could cry out or take aim or even wholly regain his balance, the second shot rang out. He swayed, and toppled, and fell against a tree in a half-sitting posture, quite dead. It struck David as an odd sight to be in a bright patch of the sun. A chicken came wandering in to share it with him. It seemed unsteady on its legs, a little dazed. He recognized it as the one which had fled wildly down the road. Forlorn thing. With kindly, absorbing pleasure he watched it snatch up in its beak an insect from out of the earth. Then, as if his cue had been given, he started, and gave at once the cry of a grouse.

Down around the fire a man with his coat open and white shirt showing, looked up sharply, dropped his armload of fresh wood abruptly. He said something in a low tone to the men nearest him, and five of them followed as he entered cautiously into the woods. David knew by this that they guessed it was no ordinary game bird that was calling from the thicket. And he experienced a confused and peculiar joy. When the white-shirted leader—the one who had marched away with the pig— came within hearing, David gave the soft cluck, cluck, cluck of the ruffled grouse which precedes its flight.

Evidently the other was as acquainted with the ways of the woods as he, for the Yankee stopped and listened, as if for the rustle of wings which should follow; when none came he proceeded even more guarded- ly. He was within range now, but David did not fire. His hesitation was due more to an inbred code of respect than to any present studying over the matter—the fellow was no addlepate, and he deserved a chance.

David waited. He could see now that the white-shirted one still had down on his cheeks, and zest in him for everything. Suddenly he raised his head and their eyes met. There was the shock for a second of an actual contact. Then, the vibration still in his arms, his legs, his chest, David presented his musket. But the lock hung up and it would not fire. He jerked and yanked. The whole world was a confusion of blue cloth and shining metal. There was no moisture in David's mouth, and he could not swallow. He heard distinctly the preliminary click of the Federal trigger. There flashed in his mind all the things a man about to die should think of, but there was no time.

The splintering, crackling sounds were the sycamore branches breaking as he fell down through them, and the sound of the impact of the body on the earth was a peculiar mingling of something dead and something deeply living.

The boy in blue stood with his carbine hanging loosely from his right hand, his mouth open, the oppression so great within him he could not breathe properly.

"See," he pointed tragically as the others came up, "see what I've done!"

In amazement, derision, four of them heard him. But the fifth, an old man who had lived long and knew much, was silent. He kicked the chicken away from the new puddle of entrails.

Bayou l'Ombre: An Incident of the War

Grace King

OF COURSE THEY knew all about war—soldiers, flags, music, generals on horseback brandishing swords, knights in armor escalading walls, cannons booming through clouds of smoke. They were familiarized with it pictorially and by narrative long before the alphabet made its appearance in the nursery with rudimentary accounts of the world they were born into, the simple juvenile world of primary sensations and colors. Their great men, and great women, too, were all fighters; the great events of their histories, battles; the great places of their geography, where they were fought (and generally the more bloody the battle, the more glorious the place); while their little chronology—the pink-covered one—stepped briskly over the centuries solely on the names of kings and sanguinary saliencies. Sunday added the sabbatical supplement to week-day lessons, symbolizing religion, concreting sin, incorporating evil, for their better comprehension, putting Jehovah himself in armor, to please their childish faculties—the omnipotent Intervener of the Old Testament, for whom they waved banners, sang hymns, and by

the brevet title, "little *soldiers* of the cross," felt committed as by bap-
tism to an attitude of expectant hostility. Mademoiselle Couper, their
governess, eased the cross-stitching in their samplers during the evenings, after supper, with traditions of "le grand Napoléon," in whose
army her grandfather was a terrible and distinguished officer, le Capitaine Césaire Paul Picquet de Montignac; and although Mademoiselle
Couper was most unlovable and exacting at times, and very homely,
such were their powers of sympathetic enthusiasm even then that they
often went to bed envious of the possessor of so glorious an ancestor, and
dreamed fairy tales of him whose gray hair, enshrined in a brooch, re-
posed comfortably under the folds of mademoiselle's fat chin—the hair
that Napoleon had looked upon!

When a war broke out in their own country they could hardly credit
their good-fortune; that is, Christine and Régina, for Lolotte was still a
baby. A wonderful panorama was suddenly unfolded before them. It
was their first intimation of the identity of the world they lived in with the
world they learned about, their first perception of the existence of an
entirely novel sentiment in their hearts—patriotism, the *amour sacré de
la patrie*, over which they had seen mademoiselle shed tears as copiously
as her grandfather had blood. It made them and all their little companions feel very proud, this war; but it gave them a heavy sense of responsibility, turning their youthful precocity incontinently away from books,
slates, and pianos towards the martial considerations that befitted the
hour. State rights, Federal limits, monitors and fortresses, proclama-
tions, Presidents, recognitions, and declarations, they acquired them all
with facility, taxing, as in other lessons, their tongue to repeat the unin-
telligible on trust for future intelligence. As their father fired his huge
after-dinner bombs, so they shot their diminutive ammunition; as he
lighted brands in the great conflagration, they lighted tapers; and the
two contending Presidents themselves did not get on their knees with
more fervor before their colossal sphinxes than these little girls did before
their doll-baby presentment of "Country." It was very hard to realize at
times that histories and story-books and poetry would indeed be written
about them; that little flags would mark battles all over the map of their
country—the country Mademoiselle Couper despised as so hopelessly,
warlessly insignificant; that men would do great things and women say
them, teachers and copy-books reiterate them, and children learn them,
just as they did of the Greeks and Romans, the English and French.

The great advantage was having God on their side, as the children of Israel had; the next best thing was having the finest country, the most noble men, and the bravest soldiers. The only fear was that the enemy would be beaten too easily, and the war cease too soon to be glorious; for, characteristic of their sex, they demanded nothing less than that their war should be the longest, bloodiest, and most glorious of all wars ever heard of, in comparison with which even "le grand Napoléon" and his Capitaine Picquet would be effaced from memory. For this were exercised their first attempts at extempore prayer. God, the dispenser of inexhaustible supplies of munitions of war, became quite a different power, a nearer and dearer personality, than "Our Father," the giver of simple daily bread, and He did not lack reminding of the existence of the young Confederacy, nor of the hearsay exigencies they gathered from the dinner-table talk.

Titine was about thirteen, Gina twelve, and Lolotte barely eight years old, when this, to them, happy break in their lives occurred. It was easily comprehensible to them that their city should be captured, and that to escape that grim ultimatum of Mademoiselle Couper, *"passées au fil de l'épée,"* they should be bundled up very hurriedly one night, carried out of their home, and journey in troublesome roundabout ways to the plantation on Bayou l'Ombre.

That was all four years ago. School and play and city life, dolls and fetes and Santa Claus, had become the property of memory. Peace for them hovered in that obscurity which had once enveloped war, while "'61," "'62," "'63," "'64," filled immeasurable spaces in their short past. Four times had Christine and Régina changed the date in their diaries—the last token of remembrance from Mademoiselle Couper—altering the numerals with naive solemnity, as if under the direction of the Almighty himself, closing with conventional ceremony the record of the lived-out twelve months, opening with appropriate aspirations the year to come. The laboriously careful chronicle that followed was not, however, of the growth of their bodies advancing by inches, nor the expansion of their minds, nor of the vague forms that began to people the shadowland of their sixteen- and seventeen-year-old hearts. Their own budding and leafing and growing was as unnoted as that of the trees and weeds about them. The progress of the war, the growth of their hatred of the enemy, the expansion of the *amour sacré* germ—these were the confidences that filled the neatly-stitched foolscap volumes. If on comparison one sister was found to have been happier in the rendition of the common sentiment, the coveted fervor and eloquence were plagiarized or imitated the next day by the other, a generous emulation thus keeping the original flame not only alight, but burning, while from assimilating each other's sentiments the two girls grew with identity of purpose into identity of mind, and effaced the slight difference of age between them.

Little Lolotte responded as well as she could to the enthusiastic exactions of her sisters. She gave her rag dolls patriotic names, obediently hated and loved as they required, and learned to recite all the war songs procurable, even to the teeming quantities of the stirring "Men of the South, our foes are up!" But as long as the squirrels gambolled on the fences, the blackbirds flocked in the fields, and the ditches filled with fish; as long as the seasons imported such constant variety of attractions—persimmons, dewberries, blackberries, acorns, wild plums, grapes, and muscadines; as long as the cows had calves, the dogs puppies, the hogs pigs, and the quarters new babies to be named; as long as the exasperating negro children needed daily subjugation, regulation, and discipline—the day's measure was too well filled and the night's slumber too short to admit of her carrying on a very vigorous warfare for a country so far away from Bayou l'Ombre—a country whose grievances she could not understand.

But—there were no soldiers, flags, music, parades, battles, or sieges. This war was altogether distinct from the wars contained in books or in Mademoiselle Couper's memory. There was an absence of the simplest requirements of war. They kept awaiting the familiar events for which they had been prepared; but after four years the only shots fired on Bayou l'Ombre were at game in the forest, the only blood shed was from the tottering herds of Texas beeves driven across the swamps to them, barely escaping by timely butchery the starvation they came to relieve, and the only heroism they had been called upon to display was still going to bed in the dark. Indeed, were it not that they knew there was a war they might have supposed that some malignant fairy had transported them from a state of wealth and luxury to the condition of those miserable Hathorns, the pariahs of their childhood, who lived just around the corner from them in the city, with whom they had never been allowed to associate. If they had not so industriously fostered the proper feelings in their hearts, they might almost have forgotten it, or, like

Lolotte, been diverted from it by the generous overtures of nature all around them. But they kept on reminding each other that it was not the degrading want of money, as in the Hathorns' case, that forced them to live on salt meat, corn-bread, and sassafras tea, to dress like the negro women in the quarters, that deprived them of education and society, and imprisoned them in a swamp-encircled plantation, the prey of chills and fever; but it was for love of country, and being little women now, they loved their country more, the more they suffered for her. Disillusion might have supervened to disappointment and bitterness have quenched hope, experience might at last have sharpened their vision, but for the imagination, that ethereal parasite which fattens on the stagnant forces of youth and garnishes with tropical luxuriance the abnormal source of its nourishment. Soaring aloft, above the prosaic actualities of the present, beyond the rebutting evidence of earth, was a fanciful stage where the drama of war such as they craved was unfolded; where neither homespun, starvation, overflows, nor illness were allowed to enter; where the heroes and heroines they loved acted roles in all the conventional glitter of costume and conduct, amid the dazzling pomps and circumstances immortalized in history and romance. Their hearts would bound and leap after these phantasms, like babes in nurses' arms after the moon, and would almost burst with longing, their ripe little hearts, Pandora-boxes packed with passions and pleasures for a lifetime, ready to spring open at a touch! On moonlit nights in summer, or under the low gray clouds of winter days, in the monotony of nothingness about them, the yearning in their breasts was like that of hunting dogs howling for the unseen game. Sometimes a rumor of a battle "out in the Confederacy" would find its way across the swamps to them, and months afterwards a newspaper would be thrown to them from a passing skiff, some old, useless, tattered, disreputable, journalistic tramp, garrulous with mendacities; but it was all true to them, if to no one else in the world—the factitious triumphs, the lurid glories, the pyrotechnical promises, prophecies, calculations, and Victory with the laurel wreath always in the future, never out of sight for an instant. They would con the fraudulent evangel, entranced; their eyes would sparkle, the blood color their cheeks, their voices vibrate, and a strange strength excite and nerve their bodies. Then would follow wakeful nights and restless days; Black Margarets, Jeanne d'Arcs, Maids of Saragossa, Katherine

Douglases, Charlotte Cordays,[1] would haunt them like the goblins of a delirium; then their prayers would become imperious demands upon Heaven, their diaries would almost break into spontaneous combustion from the incendiary material enmagazined in their pages, and the South would have conquered the world then and there could their hands but have pointed the guns and their hearts have recruited the armies. They would with mingled pride and envy read all the names, barely decipherable in the travel-stained record, from the President and Generals in big print to the diminishing insignificance of smallest-type privates; and they would shed tears, when the reaction would come a few days later, at the thought that in the whole area of typography, from the officers gaining immortality to the privates losing lives, there was not one name belonging to them; and they would ask why, of all the families in the South, precisely their father and mother should have no relations, why, of all the women in the South, they should be brotherless.

There was Beau, a too notorious guerilla captain; but what glory was to be won by raiding towns, wrecking trains, plundering transports, capturing couriers, disobeying orders, defying regulations? He was almost as obnoxious to his own as to the enemy's flag.

Besides, Beau at most was only a kind of a cousin, the son of a deceased step-sister of their father's; the most they could expect from him was to keep his undisciplined crew of "'Cadians," Indians, and swampers away from Bayou l'Ombre.

"Ah, if we were only men!" But no! They who could grip daggers and shed blood, they who teemed with all the possibilities of romance or poetry, they were selected for a passive, paltry contest against their own necessities; the endurance that would have laughed a siege to scorn ebbing away in a never-ceasing wrangle with fever and ague—willow-bark tea at odds with a malarious swamp!

---

[1]Black Margaret is not identified; "Maid of Saragossa" was Mari Augustin, a defender of the city against the French during the siege, 1808-1809. See Byron, *Childe Harolde*, I (53-56). Lady Katherine Douglas in 1436 at Blackfriars Monastery, Perth, heroically held off the assassins of King James I of Scotland by thrusting her arm where the bolt of the door was missing. Charlotte Corday was the assassin of Marat.

It was now early summer; the foliage of spring was lusty and strong, fast outgrowing tenderness and delicacy of shade, with hints of maturity already swelling the shape. The day was cloudless and warm, the dinner-hour was long past, and supper still far off. There were no appetizing varieties of menu to make meals objects of pleasant anticipation; on the contrary, they had become mournful effigies of a convivial institution of which they served at most only to recall the hours, monotonously measuring off the recurring days which passed like unlettered mileposts in a desert, with no information to give except that of transition. To-day the meal-times were so far apart as to make one believe that the sun had given up all forward motion, and intended prolonging the present into eternity. The plantation was quiet and still; not the dewy hush of early dawn trembling before the rising sun, nor the mysterious muteness of midnight, nor yet the lethargic dulness of summer when the vertical sun-rays pin sense and motion to the earth. It was the motionless, voiceless state of unnatural quietude, the oppressive consciousness of abstracted activity, which characterized those days when the whole force of Bayou l'Ombre went off into the swamps to cut timber. Days that began short-ly after one midnight and lasted to the other; rare days, when neither horn nor bell was heard for summons; when not a skiff, flat-boat, nor pirogue was left at the "gunnels";[2] when old Uncle John alone remained to represent both master and men in the cares and responsibilities de-volving upon his sex. The bayou lived and moved as usual, carrying its deceptive depths of brackish water unceasingly onward through the shadow and sunshine, rippling over the opposite low, soft banks, which seemed slowly sinking out of sight under the weight of the huge cypress-trees growing upon it. The long stretch of untilled fields back of the house, feebly kept in symmetrical proportion by crumbling fences, bared their rigid, seedless furrows in despairing barrenness to the sun, except in corner spots where a rank growth of weeds had inaugurated a reclamation in favor of barbarism. The sugar-house, superannuated and decrepit from unwholesome idleness, tottered against its own mas-sive, smokeless chimney; the surrounding sheds, stables, and smithy looked forsaken and neglected; the old blind mule peacefully slept in the shade of his once flagellated course under the corn-mill. Afar off against

---

[2]Floating wharf [Grace King's note].

the woods the huge wheel of the draining-machine rose from the under-brush in the big ditch. The patient buzzards, roosting on the branches of the gaunt, blasted gum-tree by the bayou, would raise their heads from time to time to question the loitering sun, or, slowly flapping their heavy wings, circle up into the blue sky, to fall again in lazy spirals to their watch-tower, or they would take short flights by twos and threes over the moribund plantation to see if dissolution had not yet set in, and then all would settle themselves again to brood and sleep and dream, and wait in tranquil certainty the striking of their banqueting hour.

The three girls were in the open hall-way of the plantation house, Christine reading, Régina knitting, both listlessly occupied. Like every-thing else, they were passively quiet, and, like everything else, their ap-pearance advertised an unwholesome lack of vitality, an insidious anamorphosis from an unexplained dearth or constraint. Their meagre maturity and scant development clashed abnormally with the surround-ing prodigality of insensible nature. Though tall, they were thin; they were fair, but sallow; their gentle deep eyes were reproachful and deprived-looking. If their secluded hearts ventured even in thought to-ward the plumings natural to their age, their coarse, homely, ill-fitting garments anathematized any coquettish effort or naive expression of a desire to find favor. Like the fields, they seemed hesitating on the back-ward path from cultivation. Lolotte stood before the cherry-wood armoire that held the hunting and fishing tackle, the wholesome recepta-cle of useful odds and ends. Not old enough to have come into the war with preconceptions, Lolotte had no reconciliations or compromises to effect between the ideal and the real, no compensations to solicit from an obliging imagination, which so far never rose beyond the possibilities of perch, blackbirds, and turtle eggs. The first of these occupied her thoughts at the present moment. She had made a tryst with the negro children at the draining-machine this afternoon. If she could, un-perceived, abstract enough tackle from the armoire for the crowd, and if they could slip away from the quarters, and she evade the surveillance of Uncle John, there were be a diminished number of "brim" and "goggle-eye" in the ditch out yonder, and such a notable addition to the planta-tion supper to-night as would crown the exploit a success, and establish for herself a reputation above all annoying recollections of recent mis-haps and failures. As she tied the hooks on to the lines she saw herself surrounded by the acclaiming infantile populace, pulling the struggling perch up one after the other; she saw them strung on palmetto thongs, long strings of them; she walked home at the head of her procession; heard Peggy's exclamations of surprise, smelt them frying, and finally was sitting at the table, a plate of bones before her, the radiant hostess of an imperial feast.

"Listen!" Like wood-ducks from under the water, the three heads rose simultaneously above their abstractions. "Rowlock! Rowlock!" The eyes might become dull, the tongue inert, and the heart languid on Bayou l'Ombre, but the ears were ever assiduous, ever on duty. Quivering and nervous, they listened even through sleep for that one blessed echo of travel, the signal from another and a distant world. Faint, shadowy, delusive, the whispering forerunner of on-coming news, it overrode the rippling of the current, the hooting of the owls, the barking of dogs, the splash of the gar-fish, the grunting of the alligator, the croaking of frogs, penetrating all turmoil, silencing all other sounds. "Rowlock! Rowlock!" Slow, deliberate, hard, and strenuous, coming upstream; easy, soft, and musical, gliding down. "Rowlock! Rowlock!" Every stroke a very universe of hope, every oar frothing a sea of expectation! Was it the bayou or the secret stream of their longing that suggested the sound today? "Rowlock! Rowlock!" The smouldering glances brightened in their eyes, they hollowed their hands behind their ears and held their breath for greater surety. "Rowlock! Rowlock!" In clear, distinct reiteration. It resolved the moment of doubt.

"Can it be papa coming back?"

"No; it's against stream."

"It must be swampers."

"Or hunters, perhaps."

"Or Indians from the mound."

"Indians in a skiff?"

"Well, they sometimes come in a skiff."

The contingencies were soon exhausted, a cut-off leading travellers far around Bayou l'Ombre, whose snaggy, rafted, convoluted course was by universal avoidance relegated to an isolation almost insulting. The girls, listening, not to lose a single vibration, quit their places and advanced to the edge of the gallery, then out under the trees, then to the levee, then to the "gunnels," where they stretched their long, thin, white necks out of their blue and brown check gowns, and shaded their eyes and gazed down-stream for the first glimpse of the skiff—their patience which had lasted months fretting now over the delay of a few moments.

"At last we shall get some news again."

"If they only leave a newspaper!"

"Or a letter," said Lolotte.

"A letter! From whom?"

"Ah, that's it!"

"What a pity papa isn't here!"

"Lolotte, don't shake the gunnels so; you are wetting our feet."

"How long is it since the last one passed?"

"I can tell you," said Lolotte—"I can tell you exactly: it was the day Lou Ann fell in the bayou and nearly got drowned."

"You mean when you both fell in."

"I didn't fall in at all; I held on to the pirogue."

The weeping-willow on the point below veiled the view; stretching straight out from the bank, it dropped its shock of long, green, pliant branches into the water, titillating and dimpling the surface. The rising bayou bore a freight of logs and drift from the swamps above; rudely pushing their way through the willow boughs, they tore and bruised the fragile tendrils that clung to the rough bark, scattering the tiny leaves which followed hopelessly after in their wake or danced up and down in the hollow eddies behind them. Each time the willow screen moved, the gunnels swayed under the forward motion of the eager bodies of the girls.

"At last!"

They turned their eyes to the shaft of sunlight that fell through the plantation clearing, bridging the stream. The skiff touched, entered, and passed through it with a marvellous revelation of form and color, the oars silvering and dripping diamonds, arrows and lances of light scintillating from polished steel, golden stars rising like dust from tassels, cordons, buttons, and epaulets, while the blue clouds themselves seemed to have fallen from their empyrean heights to uniform the rowers with their own celestial hue—blue, not gray!

"Rowlock! Rowlock!" What loud, frightful, threatening reverberations of the oars! And the bayou flowed on the same, and the cypress-trees gazed stolidly and steadfastly up to the heavens, and the heavens were serenely blue and white! But the earth was sympathetic, the ground shook and swayed under their feet; or was it the rush of thoughts that made their heads so giddy? They tried to arrest one and hold it for guidance, but on they sped, leaving only wild confusion of conjecture behind.

"Rowlock! Rowlock!" The rudder headed the bow for the gunnels.

"Titine! Gina! Will they kill us all?" whispered Lolotte, with anxious horror.

The agile Lou Ann, Lolotte's most efficient coadjutor and Uncle John's most successful tormentor, dropped her bundle of fishing-poles (which he had carefully spread on his roof to "cure"), and while they rolled and rattled over the dry shingles she scrambled with inconceivable haste to her corner of descent. Holding to the eaves while her excited black feet searched and found the top of the window that served as a step, she dropped into the ash-hopper below. Without pausing, as usual, to efface betraying evidences of her enterprise from her person, or to cover her tracks in the wet ashes, she jumped to the ground, and ignoring all secreting offers of bush, fence, or ditch, contrary to her custom, she ran with all the speed of her thin legs down the shortest road to the quarters. They were, as she knew, deserted. The doors of the cabins were all shut, with logs of wood or chairs propped against them. The chickens and dogs were making free of the galleries, and the hogs wallowed in peaceful immunity underneath. A waking baby from a lonely imprisoned cradle sent cries for relief through an open window. Lou Ann, looking neither to the right nor to the left, slackened not her steps, but passed straight on through the little avenue to the great white-oak which stood just outside the levee on the bank of the bayou.

Under the wide-spreading, moss-hung branches, upon the broad flat slope, a grand general washing of the clothes of the small community was in busy progress by the women, a proper feminine consecration of this purely feminine day. The daily irksome routine was broken, the men were all away, the sun was bright and warm, the air soft and sweet. The vague recesses of the opposite forest were dim and silent, the bayou played under the gunnels in caressing modulations. All furthered the hearkening and the yielding to a debonair mood, with disregard of concealment, license of pose, freedom of limb, hilarity, conviviality, audacities of heart and tongue, joyous indulgence in freak and impulse, banishment of thought, a return, indeed, for one brief moment to the wild, sweet ways of nature, to the festal days of ancestral golden age (a short retrogression for them), when the body still had claims, and the mind concessions, and the heart owed no allegiance, and when god and satyr eyes still might be caught peeping and glistening from leafy covert on feminine midsummer gambols. Their skirts were girt high around their broad full hips, their dark arms and necks came naked out of their low, sleeveless, white chemise bodies, and glistened with perspiration in the sun as if frosted with silver. Little clouds of steam rose from the kettles standing around them over heaps of burning chips. The splay-legged battling-boards sank firmer and firmer into the earth under the blows of the bats, pounding and thumping the wet clothes, squirting the warm suds in all directions, up into the laughing faces, down into the panting bosoms, against the shortened, clinging skirts, over the bare legs, out in frothy runnels over the soft red clay corrugated with innumerable toe-prints. Out upon the gunnels the water swished and foamed under the vigorous movements of the rinsers, endlessly bending and raising their flexible, muscular bodies, burying their arms to the shoulders in the cool, green depths, piling higher and higher the heaps of tightly-wrung clothes at their sides. The water-carrier, passing up and down the narrow, slippery plank-way, held the evenly filled pails with the ease of coronets upon their heads. The children, under compulsion of continuous threats and occasional chastisement, fed the fire with chips from distant wood-piles, squabbling for the possession of the one cane-knife to split kindlers, imitating the noise and echoing with absurd fidelity the full-throated laughter that interrupted from time to time the work around the wash-kettles.

High above the slop and tumult sat old Aunt Mary, the official sick-nurse of the plantation, commonly credited with conjuring powers. She held a corn-cob pipe between her yellow protruding teeth, and her little restless eyes travelled inquisitively from person to person as if in quest of professional information, twinkling with amusement at notable efforts of wit, and with malice at the general discomfiture expressed under their gaze. Heelen sat near, nursing her baby. She had taken off her kerchief, and leaned her uncovered head back against the trunk of the tree; the long wisps of wool, tightly wrapped in white knitting-cotton, rose from irregular sections all over her elongated narrow skull, and encircled her wrinkled, nervous, toothless face like some ghastly serpentine chevelure.

"De Yankees! de Yankees! I seed 'em—at de big house! Little mistus she come for Uncle John. He fotched his gun—for to shoot 'em."

Lou Ann struggled to make her exhausted breath carry all her tidings. After each item she closed her mouth and swallowed violently, working her muscles until her little horns of hair rose and moved with the contortions of her face.

"An' dey locked a passel o' men up in de smoke-house—Cornfedrits."

The bats paused in the air, the women on the gunnels lifted their arms out of the water, those on the gang-plank stopped where they were; only the kettles simmered on audibly.

Lou Ann recommenced, this time finishing in one breath, with the added emphasis of raising her arm and pointing in the direction from whence she came, her voice getting shriller and shriller to the end:

"I seed 'em. Dey was Yankees. Little mistus she come for Uncle John; he fotched his gun for to shoot 'em; and they locked a passel o' men up in de smoke-house—Cornfedrits."

The Yankees! What did it mean to them? How much from the world outside had penetrated into the unlettered fastnesses of their ignorance? What did the war mean to them? Had Bayou l'Ombre indeed isolated both mind and body? Had the subtle time-spirit itself been diverted from them by the cut-off? Could their rude minds draw no inferences from the gradual loosening of authority and relaxing of discipline? Did they neither guess nor divine their share in the shock of battle out there? Could their ghost-seeing eyes not discern the martyr-spirits rising from two opposing armies, pointing at, beckoning to them? If, indeed, the water-shed of their destiny was forming without their knowledge as without their assistance, could not maternal instinct spell it out of the heart-throbs pulsing into life under their bosoms, or read from the dumb faces of the children at their breast the triumphant secret of their superiority over others born and nourished before them?

Had they, indeed, no gratifications beyond the physical, no yearnings, no secret burden of a secret prayer to God, these bonded wives and mothers? Was this careless, happy, indolent existence genuine, or only a fool's motley to disguise a tragedy of suffering? What to them was the difference between themselves and their mistresses? their condition? or their skin, that opaque black skin which hid so well the secrets of life, which could feel but not own the blush of shame, the pallor of weakness.

If their husbands had brought only rum from their stealthy midnight excursions to distant towns, how could the child repeat it so glibly—"Yankees—Cornfedrits"? The women stood still and silent, but their eyes began to creep around furtively, as if seeking degrees of complicity in a common guilt, each waiting for the other to confess comprehension, to assume the responsibility of knowledge.

The clear-headed children, profiting by the distraction of attention from them, stole away for their fishing engagement, leaving cane-knife and chips scattered on the ground behind them. The murmuring of the bayou seemed to rise louder and louder; the cries of the forsaken baby, clamorous and hoarse, fell distinctly on the air.

"My Gord A'mighty!"

The exclamation was uncompromising; it relieved the tension and encouraged rejoinder.

"My Lord!—humph!"

One bat slowly and deliberately began to beat again—Black Maria's. Her tall, straight back was to them, but, as if they saw it, they knew that her face was settling into that cold, stern rigidity of hers, the keen eyes beginning to glisten, the long, thin nostrils nervously to twitch, the lips to open over her fine white teeth—the expression they hated and feared.

"O-h! o-h! o-h!"

A long, thin, tremulous vibration, a weird, haunting note: what inspiration suggested it?

"Glo-o-o-ry!"

Old Aunt Mary nodded her knowing head affirmatively, as if at the fulfilment of a silent prophecy. She quietly shook the ashes out of her pipe, hunted her pocket, put it in, and rising stiffly from the roof, hobbled away on her stick in the direction of her cabin.

"Glo-o-ry!"

Dead-arm Harriet stood before them, with her back to the bayou, her right arm hanging heavy at her side, her left extended, the finger pointing to the sky. A shapely arm and tapering finger; a comely, sleek, half-nude body; the moist lips, with burning red linings, barely parting to emit the sound they must have culled in uncanny practices. The heavy lids drooped over the large sleepy eyes, looking with languid passion from behind the thick black lashes.

"Glo-o-ry!" It stripped their very nerves and bared secret places of sensation! The "happy" cry of revival meetings—as if midnight were coming on, salvation and the mourners' bench before them, Judgment-day and fiery flames behind them, and "Sister Harriet" raising her voice

113

to call them on, on, through hand-clapping, foot-stamping, shouting, groaning, screaming, out of their sins, out of their senses, to rave in religious inebriation, and fall in religious catalepsy across the floor at the preacher's feet. With a wild rush, the hesitating emotions of the women sought the opportune outlet, their hungry blood bounding and leaping for the mid-day orgy. Obediently their bodies began the imperceptible motion right and left, and the veins in their throats to swell and stand out under their skins, while the short, fierce, intense responsive exclamations fell from their lips to relieve their own and increase the exaltation of the others.

"Sweet Christ! sweet Christ!"

"Take me, Saviour!"

"Oh, de Lamb! de Lamb!"

"I'm a-coming! I'm a-coming!"

"Hold back, Satan! we's a-catching on!"

"De blood's a-dripping! de blood's a-dripping!"

"Let me kiss dat cross! let me kiss it!"

"Sweet Master!"

"Glo-o-ry! Fre-e-dom!" It was a whisper, but it came like a crash, and transfixed them; their mouths stood open with the last words, their bodies remained bent to one side or the other, the febrile light in their eyes burning as if from their blood on fire. They could all remember the day when Dead-arm Harriet, the worst worker and most violent tongue of the gang, stood in the clearing, and raising that dead right arm over her head, cursed the overseer riding away in the distance. The wind had been blowing all day; there was a sudden loud crack above them, and a limb from a deadened tree broke, sailed, poised, and fell crashing to her shoulder, and deadening her arm forever. They looked instinctively now with a start to the oak above them, to the sky—only moss and leaves and blue and white clouds. And still Harriet's voice rose, the words faster, louder, bolder, more determined, whipping them out of their awe, driving them on again down the incline of their own passions.

"Glory! Freedom! Freedom! Glory!"

"I'm bound to see 'em! Come along!"

Heelen's wild scream rang shrill and hysterical. She jerked her breast from the sucking lips, and dropped her baby with a thud on the ground. They all followed her up the levee, pressing one after the other, slipping in the wet clay, struggling each one not to be left behind. Emmeline, the wife of little Ben, the only yellow woman on the place, was the last. Her skirt was held in a grip of iron; blinded, obtuse, she pulled forward, reaching her arms out after the others.

"You stay here!"

She turned and met the determined black face of her mother-in-law.

"You let me go!" she cried, half sobbing, half angry.

"You stay here, I tell you!" The words were muttered through clinched teeth.

"You let me go, I tell you!"

"Glory! Freedom!"

The others had already left the quarters, and were on the road. They two were alone on the bank now, except Heelen's baby, whimpering under the tree; their blazing eyes glared at each other. The singing voices grew fainter and fainter. Suddenly the yellow face grew dark with the surge of blood underneath, the brows wrinkled, and the lips protruded in a grimace of animal rage. Grasping her wet bat tightly with both hands, she turned with a furious bound, and raised it with all the force of her short muscular arms. The black woman darted to the ground; the cane-knife flashed in the air and came down pitilessly towards the soft fleshy shoulder. A wild, terrified scream burst from Emmeline's lips; the bat dropped; seizing her skirt with both hands, she pulled forward, straining her back out of reach of the knife; the homespun tore, and she fled up the bank, her yellow limbs gleaming through the rent left by the fragment in the hand of the black woman.

The prisoners were so young, so handsome, so heroic; the very incarnation of the holy spirit of patriotism in their pathetic uniform of brimless caps, ragged jackets, toeless shoes, and shrunken trousers—a veteran equipment of wretchedness out of keeping with their fresh young faces. How proud and unsubdued they walked through the hall between the file of bayonets! With what haughty, defiant eyes they returned the gaze of their insultingly resplendent conquerors! Oh, if girls' souls had been merchantable at that moment! Their hands tied behind their backs like runaway slaves! Locked up in the smoke-house! that dark, rancid, gloomy, mouldy depot of empty hogsheads, barrels, boxes, and fetid exhalations.

They were the first soldiers in gray the girls had ever seen; their own chivalrous knights, the champions of their radiant country. What was the story of their calamity? Treacherously entrapped? Overpowered by numbers? Where were their companions—staring with mute, cold, up-turned faces from pools of blood? And were these to be led helplessly tethered into captivity, imprisoned; with ball and chain to gangrene and disgrace their strong young limbs, or was solitary confinement to starve their hearts and craze their minds, holding death in a thousand loath-some, creeping shapes ever threateningly over them?

The smoke-house looked sinister and inimical after its sudden promo-tion from keeper of food to keeper of men. The great square white-washed logs seemed to settle more ponderously on the ground around them, the pointed roof to press down as if the air of heaven were an emissary to be dreaded; the hinges and locks were so ostentatiously mas-sive and incorruptible. What artful, what vindictive security of carpen-ter and locksmith to exclude thieves or immure patriots!

The two eldest girls stood against the open armoire with their chill fingers interlaced. Beyond the wrinkled back of Uncle John's copperas-dyed coat before them lay the region of brass buttons and blue cloth and hostility; but they would not look at it; they turned their heads away; the lids of their eyes refused to lift and reveal the repugnant vision to them. If their ears had only been equally sensitive!

"And so you are the uncle of the young ladies? Brother of the father or mother?" What clear, incisive, nasal tones! Thank Heaven for the difference between them of the voice at least!

The captain's left arm was in a sling, but his hand could steadily hold the note-book in which he carefully pencilled Uncle John's answers to his minute cross-examination—a dainty, fragrant, Russia-leather note-book, with monogram and letters and numbers emblazoned on the out-side in national colors. It had photographs inside, also, which he would pause and admire from time to time, reading the tender dedications aloud to his companions.

"And the lady in the kitchen called mammy? She is the mother, I guess?"

"P-p-p-peggy's a nigger, and my mistresses is white," stuttered Un-cle John.

"Ah, indeed! Gentlemen in my uniform find it difficult to remember these trifling distinctions of color."

What tawdry pleasantry! What hypocritical courtesy! What exqui-site ceremony and dainty manual for murderous dandies!

"Ef-ef-ef-ef I hadn't done gone and forgot dem caps!"

116

Uncle John stood before his young mistresses erect and determined, his old double-barrel shotgun firmly clasped in his tremulous hands, his blear, bloodshot eyes fearlessly measuring the foe. If it were to be five hundred lashes on his bare back under the trees out there (terms on which he would gladly have compromised), or, his secret fear, a running noose over one of the branches, or the murderous extravagance of powder and shot for him, he had made up his mind, despite every penalty, to fulfil his duty and stand by his word to Marse John. Ever since the time the little crawling white boy used to follow the great awkward black boy around like a shadow, John had made a cult of Marse John. He had taught him as a child to fish, hunt, trap birds, to dress skins, knit gloves, and play cards on the sly, to fight cocks on Sunday, to stutter, to cut the "pigeon wing" equal to any negro in the State—and other personal accomplishments besides. He had stood by him through all his scrapes as a youth, was valet to all his frolics as a young man, and now in his old age he gardened for him, and looked after the young ladies for him, stretching or contracting his elastic moral code as occasion required; but he had never deceived him nor falsified his word to him. He knew all about the war: Marse John had told him. He knew what Marse John meant when he left the children to him, and Marse John knew what to expect from John. He would treat them civilly as long as they were civil, but his gun was loaded, both barrels with bullets, and—

"Ef-ef-ef-ef I hadn't done gone and forgot dem caps!"

There was his powder-horn under one arm, there was his shot-flask filled with the last batch of slugs under the other; but the caps were not in his right-hand coat-pocket, they were in his cupboard, hidden for safety under a pile of garden "truck."

The busy martins twittered in and out of their little lodge under the eaves of the smoke-house. Régina and Christine were powerless to prevent furtive glances in that direction. Could the *prisoners* hear it inside? Could *they* see the sun travelling westward, crack by crack, chink by chink, in the roof? Could they feel it sinking, and with it sinking all their hopes of deliverance? Or did they hope still?

Maidens had mounted donjon towers at midnight, had eluded Argus-eyed sentinels, had drugged savage blood-hounds, had crossed lightning-flashed seas, had traversed robber-infested forests; whatever maidens had done they would do, for could ever men more piteously implore release from castle keep than these gray-clad youths from the smoke-house? And did ever maiden hearts beat more valiantly than theirs? (and did ever maiden limbs tremble more cowardly?) Many a tedious day had been lightened by their rehearsal of just such a drama as this; they had prepared roles for every imaginable sanguinary circumstance, but prevision, as usual, had overlooked the unexpected. The erstwhile feasible conduct, the erstwhile feasible weapons, of a Jeanne d'Arc or Charlotte Corday, the defiant speeches, the ringing retorts—how inappropriate, inadequate, here and now! If God would only help them! but, like the bayou, the cypresses, and the blue sky, He seemed to-day eternally above such insignificant human necessities as theirs.

Without the aid of introspection or the fear of capital punishment, Lolotte found it very difficult to maintain the prolonged state of rigidity into which her sisters had frozen themselves. All the alleviations devised during a wearisome experience of compulsory attendance on plantation funerals were exhausted in the course of this protracted, hymnless, prayerless solemnity. She stood wedged in between them and the armoire which displayed all its shelves of allurements to her. There were her bird-traps just within reach; there was the fascinating bag of nux-vomica root—crow poison; there was the little old work-box filled with ammunition, which she was forbidden to touch, and all the big gar-fish lines and harpoons and decoy-ducks. There were her own perch lines, the levy she had raised in favor of her companions; they were neatly rolled, ready to tie on the rods, only needing sinkers; and there was the old Indian basket filled with odds and ends, an unfailing treasure of resource and surprise. She was just about searching in it for sinkers when this interruption occurred.

The sky was so bright over the fields! Just the evening to go fishing, whether they caught anything or not. If the enemy would only hurry and go, there might still be time; they would leave, they said, as soon as mammy cooked them something to eat. She had seen mammy chasing a chicken through the yard. She wondered how the nice, fat little round "doodles"[3] were getting on in their tin can under the house; she never had had such a fine box of bait; she wondered if the negro children

---

[3]Doodles or doodle-bugs, the larvae of various insects, especially the ant lion, are used for bait.

would go all the same without her; she wondered if she could see them creeping down the road. How easy she could have got away from Uncle John! Anything almost would do for sinkers—bits of iron, nails; they had to do since her father and Uncle John made their last moulding of bullets. She thought they might have left her just one real sinker simply as a matter of distinction between herself and the little darkies. Her eyes kept returning to the Indian basket, and if she stopped twisting her fingers one over the other but a moment they would take their way to rummaging among the rusty contents.

"Glory! Freedom!"

In came the negresses, Bacchantes drunk with the fumes of their own hot blood, Dead-arm Harriet, like a triumphant sorceress, leading them, waving and gesticulating with her one "live" arm, all repeating over and over again the potent magical words, oblivious of the curious looks of the men, their own exposure, the presence of their mistresses, of everything but their own ecstasy.

"Freedom! Master! Freedom!"

Christine and Régina raised their heads and looked perplexed at the furious women in the yard, and the men gazing down to them.

What was the matter with them? What did they mean? What was it all about?

"Freedom! Freedom!"

Then light broke upon them; their fingers tightened in each other's clasp, and their cheeks flushed crimson.

"How dared they? What insolence! What—"

The opposite door stood open; they rushed across the hall and closed it between them and the humiliating scene. This, this they had not thought of, this they had never read about, this their imagination in wildest flights had not ventured upon. This was not a superficial conflict to sweep the earth with cannons and mow it with sabres; this was an earthquake which had rent it asunder, exposing the quivering organs of hidden life. What a chasm was yawning before them! There was no need to listen one to the other; the circumstances could wring from the hearts of millions but one sentiment, the tongue was left no choice of words.

"Let them go! let them be driven out! never, never to see them again!"

The anger of outraged affection, betrayed confidence, abandoned trust, traitorous denial, raged within them.

There were their servants, their possessions! From generation to generation their lives had been woven together by the shuttle of destiny. How flimsy and transparent the fabric! how grotesque and absurd the tapestry, with its vaunted traditions of mutual loyalty and devotion! What a farce, what a lying, disgusting farce it had all been! Well, it was over now; that was a comfort—all over, all ended. If the hearts had intergrown, they were torn apart now. After this there was no return, no reconciliation possible! Through the storm of their emotions a thought drifted, then another; little detached scenes flitted into memory; familiar gestures, speeches, words, one reminiscence drawing another. Thicker and thicker came little episodes of their pastoral existence together; the counter interchanges of tokens, homely presents, kind offices, loving remembrances; the mutual assistance and consolation in all the accidents of life traversed together, the sicknesses, the births, the deaths; and so many thousand trivial incidents of long, long ago—memory had not lost one—down to the fresh eggs and the pop-corn of that very morning; they were all there, falling upon their bruised hearts.

In the hearts of the women out there were only shackles and scourges. What of the long Sundays of Bible-reading and catechism, the long evenings of woodland tales; the confidences; the half-hours around the open fireplaces when supper was cooking, the potatoes under their hillocks of ashes, the thin-legged ovens of cornbread with their lids of glowing coals, the savory skillets of fried meat, the—Was it indeed all of the past, never again to be present or future? And those humble, truthful, loving eyes, which had looked up to them from the first moment of their lives; did they look with greater trust up to God Himself? It was all over, yes, all over! The color faded from their faces, the scornful resolution left their lips; they laid their faces in their hands and sobbed.

"Do you hear, Titine?" Lolotte burst into the room. "They are all going to leave, every one of them; a transport is coming to-night to take them off. They are going to bundle up their things and wait at the steamboat-landing; and they are not going to take a child, and not a single husband. The captain says the government at Washington will give them the nicest white husbands in the land; that they ought to be glad to marry them. They carried on as if they were drunk. Do you believe it, Titine? Oh, I do wish Jeff Davis would hurry up and win!"

The door opened again; it was Black Maria, still holding the cane-knife in her hand. She crossed the room with her noiseless barefooted tread, and placed herself behind them. They did not expect her to say anything; Black Maria never talked much; but they understood her, as they always did.

Her skirts were still tied up, her head-kerchief awry; they saw for the first time that the wool under it was snow-white.

Black Maria! They might have known it! They looked at her. No! She was not! She was not negro, like the others. Who was she? What was she? Where did she come from, with her white features and white nature under her ebon skin? What was the mystery that enveloped her? Why did the brain always torture itself in surmises about her? Why did she not talk as the others did, and just for a moment uncover that coffin heart of hers? Why was she, alone of all the negroes, still an alien, a foreigner, an exile among them? Was she brooding on disgrace, outrage, revenge? Was she looking at some mirage behind her—a distant equatorial country, a princely rank, barbaric state, some inherited memory transmitted by that other Black Maria, her mother? Who was the secret black father whom no one had discovered? Was it, as the negroes said, the Prince of Darkness? Who was her own secret consort, the father of Ben? What religion had she to warrant her scornful repudiation of Christianity? What code that enabled her to walk as if she were free through slavery, to assume slavery now when others hailed freedom, to be loyal in the midst of treason?

"Look!" Lolotte came into the room, and held up a rusty, irregular piece of iron. "I found this in the old Indian basket where I was looking for sinkers. Don't you see what it is? It is the old key of the smoke-house, and I am going to let those Confederates out." She spoke quietly and decidedly. There was something else in the other hand, concealed in the folds of her dress. She produced it reluctantly. It was the gun-wrench that filled so prominent a part in her active life—always coveting it, getting possession of it, being deprived of it, and accused unfailingly for its every absence and misplacement. "You see, it is so convenient; it screws so nicely on to everything," she continued, apologetically, as she demonstrated the useful qualification by screwing it on to the key. "There! it is as good as a handle. All they've got to do is to slip away in the skiff while the others are eating. And I would like to know how they can ever be caught, without another boat on the place! But oh, girls"—her black eyes twinkled maliciously—"what fools the Yankees are!"

If the Federals, as they announced, were only going to remain long enough for the lady in the kitchen to prepare them something to eat, the length of their stay clearly rested in Peggy the cook's hands, as she understood it. She walked around her kitchen with a briskness rarely permitted by her corpulent proportions, and with an intuitive faith in the common nature of man regardless of political opinion, she exerted her culinary skill to the utmost. She knew nothing of the wholesale quarrelling and fighting of a great war, but during her numerous marital experiments, not counting intermittent conjugalities for twenty-five years with Uncle John, she had seen mercy and propitiation flow more than once after a good meal from the most irate; and a healthy digestion aiding, she never despaired of even the most revengeful. The enemy, in her opinion, were simply to be treated like furious husbands, and were to be offered the best menu possible under the trying circumstances. She worked, inspired by all the wife-lore of past ages, the infiltrated wisdom that descends to women in the course of a world of empirical connubiality, that traditionary compendium to their lives by which they still hope to make companionship with men harmonious and the earth a pleasant abiding-place. With minute particularity Peggy set the table and placed the dishes. The sun was now sinking, and sending almost horizontal rays over the roof of the smoke-house, whose ugly square frame completely blocked the view of the dining-room window. Peggy carefully drew the red calico curtain across it, and after a moment's rehearsal to bring her features to the conventional womanly expression of cheerful obtuseness to existing displeasure, she opened the dining-room door.

Gina and Lolotte stood close under the window against the dwelling, looking at the locked door of the smoke-house before them, listening to the sounds falling from the dining-room above. Once in the skiff, the prisoners were safe; but the little red curtain of the window fluttering flimsily in the breeze coquetted with their hopes and the lives of three men. If the corners would but stay down a second! Titine and Black Maria were in front, busy about the skiff. Peggy's culinary success appeared, from the comments of the diners, to be complimentary to her judgment. But food alone, however, does not suffice in the critical moments of life; men are half managed when only fed. There was another menu, the ingredients of which were not limited or stinted by blockade of war. Peggy had prepared that also; and in addition to the sounds of plates, knives, forks, and glasses, came the tones of her rich voice dropping from a quick tongue the *entremets* of her piquant imagination. The attention in the room seemed tense, and at last the curtain hung straight and motionless.

"Now! now!" whispered Gina. "We must risk something."

Woman-like, they paused midway and looked back; a hand stretched from the table was carelessly drawing the curtain aside, and the window stared unhindered at the jail.

Why had they waited? Why had they not rushed forward immediately? By this time their soldiers might have been free! They could hear Peggy moving around the table; they could see her bulky form push again and again across the window.

"Mammy! Mammy!"

Could she hear them? They clasped their hands and held their faces up in imploring appeal. The sun was setting fast, almost running down the west to the woods. The dinner, if good, was not long. It all depended upon Peggy now.

"Mammy! Mammy!" They raised their little voices, then lowered them in agony of apprehension. "Mammy, do something! Help us!"

But still she passed on and about, around the table, and across the window, blind to the smoke-house, deaf to them, while her easy, familiar voice recited the comical gyrations of "old Frizzly," the half-witted hen, who had set her heart against being killed and stewed, and ran and hid, and screamed and cackled, and ducked and flew, and then, after her silly head was twisted off, "just danced, as if she were at a "Cadian' ball, all over the yard."

It would soon be too late! It was, perhaps, too late now!

Black Maria had got the skiff away from the gunnels, but they might just as well give it up; they would not have time enough now.

"Mammy!" The desperate girls made a supreme effort of voice and look. The unctuous black face, the red bead ear-rings, the bandanna head-kerchief, appeared at the window with "old Frizzly's" last dying cackle. There was one flashing wink of the left eye.

Her nurslings recognized then her *piéce de résistance oratoire*—a side-splitting prank once played upon her by another nursling, her pet, her idol, the plague of her life—Beau.

Who could have heard grating lock or squeaking hinges through the boisterous mirth that followed? Who could have seen the desperate bound of the three imprisoned soldiers for liberty through that screen of sumptuous flesh—the magnificent back of Mammy that filled to over-lapping the insignificant little window?

They did not wait to hear the captain's rapturous toast to Peggy in sassafras tea, nor his voluble protestations of love to her, nor could they see him in his excitement forgetting his wounded arm, bring both clinched fists with a loud bravo to the table, and then faint dead away.

"I knew it!"

"Just like him!"

"Take him in the air—quick!"

"No, sir! You take him in there, and put him on the best bed in the house." Peggy did not move from the window, but her prompt command turned the soldiers from the door in the hall, and her finger directed them to the closed bed-chamber.

Without noticing Christine standing by the open window, they dropped their doughty burden—boots, spurs, sword, epaulets, and all—on the fresh, white little bed, the feather mattress fluffing up all around as if to submerge him.

"Oh, don't bother about that; cut the sleeve off!"

"Who has a knife?"

"There."

"That's all right now."

"He's coming round."

"There's one nice coat spoiled."

"Uncle Sam has plenty more."

"Don't let it drip on the bed."

"Save it to send to Washington—trophy—wet with rebel blood."

The captain was evidently recovering.

"You stay here while I keep 'em eating," whispered Peggy, authoritatively, to Christine.

Titine trembled as if she had an ague.

"How could they help seeing the tall form of Black Maria standing in the prow of the boat out in the very middle of the bayou? Suppose she, Titine, had not been there to close the window quick as thought? Suppose instead of passing through her room she had run through the basement, as she intended, after pushing off the skiff?"

Rollicking, careless, noisy, the soldiers went back to their interrupted meal, while the boat went cautiously down the bayou to the meeting place beyond the clearing.

"How far was Black Maria now?" Titine opened the window a tiny crack. "Heavens! how slowly she paddled! lifting the oar deliberately from side to side, looking straight ahead. How clear and distinct she was in the soft evening light! Why did she not hurry? why did she not row? She could have muffled the oars. But no, no one thought of that; that was always the way—always something overlooked and forgotten. The soldiers could finish a dozen dinners before the skiff got out of sight at this rate. Without the skiff the prisoners might just as well be locked still in the smoke-house. Did he on the bed suspect something, seeing her look out this way?" She closed the window tight.

"How dark the room was! She could hardly see the wounded man. How quiet he was! Was he sleeping, or had he fainted again? In her bed! her enemy lying in her bed! his head on her pillow, her own little pillow, the feverish confidant of so many sleepless nights! How far were they now on the bayou? She must peep out again. Why, Maria had not moved! not moved an inch! Oh, if she could only scream to her! if she were only in the skiff!

"How ghastly pale he looked on the bed! his face as white as the coverlet, his hair and beard so black; how changed without his bravado and impertinence! And he was not old, either; not older than the boys in gray. She had fancied that age and ugliness alone could go with violence and wrong. How much gold! how much glitter! Why, the sun did not rise with more splendor of equipment. Costumed as if for the conquest of worlds. If the Yankees dressed their captains this way, what was the livery of their generals? How curious the sleeveless arm looked! What a horrible mark the gash made right across the soft white skin! What a scar it would leave! What a disfigurement! And this, this is what men call love of country!"

On Saturday nights sometimes, in the quarters, when rum had been smuggled in, the negroes would get to fighting and beating their wives, and her father would be sent for in a hurry to come with his gun and separate them. Hatchets, axes, cane-knives—anything they would seize, to cut and slash one another, husbands, wives, mothers, sons, sisters, brothers; but they were negroes, ignorant, uneducated, barbarous, excited; they could not help it; they could not be expected to resist all at once the momentum of centuries of ancestral ferocity. But for white men, gentlemen, thus furiously to mar and disfigure their own mother-given bodies! All the latent maternal instinct in her was roused, all the woman in her revolted against the sacrilegious violence of mutilation. "Love of country to make her childless, or only the mother of invalids! This was only one. What of the other thousands and hundreds of thousands? Are men indeed so inexhaustible? Are the pangs of maternity so cheap? Are women's hearts of no account whatever in the settlement of disputes? O God! cannot the world get along without war? But even if men want it, even if God permits it, how can the women allow it? If the man on the bed were a negro, she could do something for his arm. Many a time, early Sunday mornings, Saturday night culprits had come to her secretly, and she had washed off the thick, gummy blood, and bandaged up their cuts and bruises; they did not show so on black skin.... This man had a mother somewhere among the people she called 'enemies'; a mother sitting counting day by day the continued possession of a live son, growing gray and old before that terrible next minute ever threatening to take her boy and give her a corpse. Or perhaps, like her own, his mother might be dead. They might be friends in that kingdom which the points of the compass neither unite nor divide; together they might be looking down on this quarrelling, fighting world; mothers, even though angels, looking, looking through smoke and powder and blood and hatred after their children. Their eyes might be fixed on this lonely little spot, on this room...." She walked to the bed.

The blood was oozing up through the strips of plaster. She stanched and bathed and soothed the wound as she well knew how with her tender, agile fingers, and returned to the window. Maria had disappeared now; she could open the window with impunity. The trackless water was flowing innocently along, the cooling air was rising in mist, the cypress-trees checked the brilliant sky with the filigree and net-work of their bristly foliage. The birds twittered, the chickens loitered and dallied on their way to roost. The expectant dogs were lying on the levee waiting for the swampers, who, they ought to know, could not possibly return before midnight. And Molly was actually on time this evening, lowing for mammy to come and milk her; what was the war to her? How happy and peaceful it all was! What a jarring contrast to swords and bayonets! Thank God that Nature was impartial, and could not be drilled into partisanship! If humanity were like Nature! If—if there had been no war! She paused, shocked at her first doubt; of the great Circumstance of her life it was like saying, "If there had been no God!"

As she stood at the window and thought, all the brilliant coloring of her romantic fantasies, the stories of childhood, the perversions of education, the self-delusions, they all seemed to fade with the waning light, and with the beautiful day sink slowly and quietly into the irrevocable past. "Thank God, above all, that it is a human device to uniform people into friends and enemies! The heart (her own felt so soft and loving)—the heart repudiates such attempts of blue and gray; it still clings to Nature, and belongs only to God." She thought the wound must need tending again, and returned to the bed. The patient, meanwhile, went in and out of the mazes of unconsciousness caused by weakness.

"Was that really he on this foamy bed? What a blotch his camp-battered body made down the centre of it! It was good to be on a bed once more, to look up into a mosquito-bar instead of the boughs of trees, to feel his head on a pillow. But why did they put him there? Why did they not lay him somewhere on the floor, outside on the ground, instead of soiling and crumpling this lily-white surface?"

He could observe his nurse through his half-closed lids, which fell as she approached the bed, and closed tight as she bent above him. When she stood at the window he could look full at her. "How innocent and unsuspecting she looked!" The strained rigidity had passed away from her face. Her transparent, child-like eyes were looking with all their life of expression in the direction of the bed, and then at something passing in her own mind. "Thank Heaven, the fright had all gone out of them! How horrible for a gentleman to read fear in the eyes of a woman! Her mind must be as pure and white, yes, and as impressionable, too, as her bed. Did his presence lie like a blot upon it also? How she must hate him! how she must loathe him! Would it have been different if he had come in the other uniform—if he had worn the gray? would she then have cared for him, have administered to him? How slight and frail she was! What a wan, wistful little face between him and the gloomy old bayou! He could see her more plainly now since she had opened the window and let in the cool, fragrant air. There was no joyous development of the body in her to proclaim womanhood, none of the seductive, confident beauty that follows coronation of youth; to her had only come the care and anxiety of maturity. This—this," he exclaimed to himself, "is the way women fight a war." Was she coming this way? Yes. To the bed? Hardly. Now she was pressing against it, now bending over him, now dropping a cooling dew from heaven on his burning arm, and now—oh, why so soon? she was going away to stand and look out of the window again.

The homely little room was filled with feminine subterfuges for ornament, feminine substitutes for comfort. How simple women are! how little they require, after all! only peace and love and quiet, only the impossible in a masculine world. What was she thinking of? If he could only have seen the expression of her eyes as she bent over him! Suppose he should open his and look straight up at her? but no, he had not the courage to frighten her again. He transplanted her in his mind to other surroundings, her proper surroundings by birthright, gave her in abundance all of which this war had deprived her, presented to her assiduous courtiers, not reckless soldiers like himself, but men whom peace had guided in the lofty sphere of intellectual pursuits. He held before her the sweet invitations of youth, the consummations of life. He made her smile, laugh.

"Ah!"—he turned his face against the pillow—"had that sad face ever laughed? Could any woman laugh during a war? Could any triumph, however glorious, atone for battles that gave men death, but left the women to live? This was only one; how many, wan and silent as she, were looking at this sunset—the sunset not of a day, but a life? When it was all over, who was to make restitution to them, the women? Was any cost too great to repurchase for them simply the privilege of hoping again? What an endless chain of accusing thoughts! What a miserable conviction tearing his heart! If he could get on his knees to her, if he could kiss her feet, if he could beg pardon in the dust—he, a man for all men, of her, a woman for all women. If he could make her his country, not to fight, but to work for, it…"

She came to his side again, she bent over him, she touched him.

Impulsive, thoughtless, hot-headed, he opened his eyes full, he forgot again the wounded arm. With both hands he stayed her frightened start; he saw the expression of her eyes bending over him.

"Can you forgive me? It is a heartless, cowardly trick! I am not a Yankee; I am Beau, your cousin, the guerilla."

The door of the smoke-house opened, the escaped soldiers ran like deer between the furrows of Uncle John's vegetable garden, where the waving corn leaves could screen them; then out to the bank of the bayou—not on the levee, but close against the fence—snagging their clothes and scratching their faces and hands on the cuckleburs;[4] Lolotte in front, with a stick in her hand, beating the bushes through habit to frighten the snakes, calling, directing, animating, in excited whispers; Régina in the rear, urging, pressing, sustaining the young soldier lagging behind, but painfully striving with stiffened limbs to keep up with the pace of his older, more vigorous companions. Ahead of them Black Maria was steadily keeping the skiff out in the current. The bayou narrowed and grew dark as it entered between the banks of serried cypress-trees, where night had already begun.

Régina looked hurriedly over her shoulder. "Had they found out yet at the house? How slowly she ran! How long it took to get to the woods! Oh, they would have time over and over again to finish their dinner and catch them. Perhaps at this very moment, as she was thinking of it, some forgotten article in the skiff was betraying them! Perhaps a gun might even now be pointing down their path! Or, now! the bullet could start and the report come too late to warn them."

She looked back again and again.

From the little cottage under the trees the curtains fluttered, but no bayonet nor smooth-bore was visible.

She met her companion's face, looking back also, but not for guns—for her. "If it had been different! If he had been a visitor, come to stay; days and evenings to be passed together!" The thought lifting the sulphurous war-clouds from her heart, primitive idyls burst into instantaneous fragrant bloom in it like spring violets. He was not only the first soldier in gray she had ever seen, but the first young man; or it seemed so to her.

Again she looked back.

"How near they were still to the house! how plainly they could yet be seen! He could be shot straight through the back, the gray jacket getting one stain, one bullet-hole, more, the country one soldier less. Would they shoot through a woman at him? Would they be able to separate them if she ran close behind him, moving this way and that way, exactly as he did? If she saw them in time she could warn him; he could lie flat down in the grass; then it would be impossible to hit him."

Increasing and narrowing the space between them at the hest of each succeeding contradictory thought, turning her head again and again to the house behind her, she lost speed. Lolotte and the two men had al-

---

[4] A cucklebur is a variant of cuckold-bur or cocklebur.

ready entered the forest before she reached it. Coming from the fields, the swamps seemed midnight dark. Catching her companion's hand, they groped their way along, tripped by the slimy cypress knees that rose like evil gnomes to beset and entangle their feet, slipping over rolling logs, sinking in stagnant mire, noosed by the coils of heavy vines that dropped from unseen branches overhead. Invisible wings of startled birds flapped above them, the croaking of frogs ebbed and flowed around them, owls shrieked and screamed from side to side of the bayou. Lolotte had ceased her beating; swamp serpents are too sluggish to be frightened away. In the obscurity, Black Maria could be dimly seen turning the skiff to a half-submerged log, from which a turtle dropped as if ballasted with lead. A giant cypress-tree arrested them; the smooth, fluted trunk, ringed with whitish water-marks, recording floods far over their heads; where they were scrambling once swam fish and serpents. The young soldier turned and faced her, the deliverer, whose manoeuvres in the open field had not escaped him.

She had saved him from imprisonment, insult, perhaps death—the only heir of a heroic father, the only son of a widowed mother; she had restored him to a precious heritage of love and honor, replaced him in the interrupted ambitious career of patriotic duty; she had exposed her life for him—she was beautiful. She stood before him, panting, tremulous, ardent, with dumb, open red lips, and voluble, passionate eyes, and with a long scratch in her white cheek from which the blood trickled. She had much to say to him, her gray uniformed hero; but how in one moment express four years—four long years—and the last long minutes. The words were all there, had been rushing to her lips all day; her lips were parted; but the eager, overcrowded throng were jammed on the threshold; and her heart beat so in her ears! He could not talk; he could not explain. His companions were already in the boat, his enemies still in gunshot. He bent his face to hers in the dim light to learn by heart the features he must never forget—closer, closer, learning, knowing more and more, with the eager precocity of youth.

Bellona must have flown disgusted away with the wings of an owl, Columbia might have nodded her head as knowingly as old Aunt Mary could, when the callow hearts, learning and knowing, brought the faces closer and closer together, until the lips touched.

"I shall come again; I shall come again. Wait for me. Surely I shall come again."

"Yes! Yes!"

Black Maria pushed the skiff off. "Rowlock! Rowlock!" They were safe and away.

A vociferous group stood around the empty gunnels. Uncle John, with the daring of desperation, advanced, disarmed as he was, towards them.

"I-I-I-I don't keer ef you is de-de-de President o' de United States hisself, I ain't gwine to 'low no such cussin' and' swearin' in de hearin' o' de-de-de young ladies. Marse John he-he-he don't 'low it, and when Marse John ain't here I-I-I don't 'low it."

His remonstrance and heroic attitude had very little effect, for the loud talk went on, and chiefly by ejaculation, imprecation, and self-accusation published the whole statement of the case; understanding which, Uncle John added his voice also:

"Good Gord A'mighty! Wh-wh-what's dat you say? Dey-dey-dey Yankees, an' you Cornfedrits? Well, sir, an' are you Marse Beau—you wid your arm hurted? Go 'long! You can't fool me; Marse Beau done had more sense en dat. My Gord! an' dey wuz Yankees? You better cuss—cussin's about all you kin do now. Course de boat's gone. You'll never ketch up wid 'em in Gord's world now. Don't come along arter me about it? 'Taint my fault. How wuz I to know? You wuz Yankees enough for me. I declar', Marse Beau, you ought to be ashamed o' yourself! You wanted to l'arn dem a lesson! I reckon dey l'arnt you one! You didn't mean 'em no harm! Humph! dey've cut dey eye-teeth, dey have! Lord! Marse Beau, I thought you done knowed us better. Did you really think we wuz a-gwine to let a passel o' Yankees take us away off our own plantation? You must done forgot us. We jes cleaned out de house for 'em, we did—clo'es, food, tobacco, rum. De young ladies 'ain't lef' a mossel for Marse John. An'—an'—an' 'fore the good Gord, my gun! Done tuck my gun away wid 'em! Wh-wh-wh-what you mean by such doin's? L-l-look here, Marse Beau, I don't like dat, nohow! Wh-w-what! you tuck my gun and gin it to the Yankees? Dat's my gun! I done had dat gun twenty-five year an' more! Dog-gone! Yes, sir, I'll cuss—I'll cuss ef I wants to! I 'ain't got no use for gorillas, nohow! Lem me 'lone, I tell you! lem me 'lone! Marse John he'll get de law o' dat! Who's 'sponsible? Dat's all I want to know—who's 'sponsible? Ef-ef-ef-ef—No, sir; dar ain't' nary boat on de place, nor hereabouts. Yes, sir; you kin cross de swamp ef you kin find de way. No, sir—no, sir; dar ain't no one to show you. I ain't gwine to leave de young ladies twell Marse John he comes back. Yes, I reckon you kin git to de cut-off by to-morrow mornin', ef you ain't shot on de way for Yankees, an' ef your company is fool enough to wait for you. No, sir, I don't know nothin' 'bout nothin'; you better wait an' arsk Marse John....My Gord! I'm obleeged to laugh; I can't help it. Dem fool nigger wimen a-sittin' on de brink o' de byer, dey clo'es tied up in de bedquilts, an' de shotes an' de pullits all kilt, a-waitin' for freedom! I lay dey'll git freedom enough to-night when de boys come home. Dey git white gentlemen to marry em! Dey'll git five hundred apiece. Marse Beau, Gord'll punish you for dis—He surely will. I done tole Marse John long time ago he oughter sell dat brazen nigger Dead-arm Harriet, an' git shet o' her. Lord! Lord! Lord! Now you done gone to cussin' and swearin' again. Don't go tearin' off your jackets an' flingin' 'em at me. We don't want 'em; we buys our clo'es—what we don't make. Yes, Marse John'll be comin' along pretty soon now. What's your hurry, Marse Beau? Well, so long ef you won't stay. He ain't got much use for gorillas neither, Marse John hain't."

The young officer wrote a few hasty words on a leaf torn from the pretty Russia-leather notebook, and handed it to the old darky. "For your Marse John."

"For Marse John—yes, sir; I'll gin hit to him soon 's he comes in."

They had dejectedly commenced their weary tramp up the bayou; he called him back, and lowered his voice confidentially: "Marse Beau, when you captured dat transport and stole all dem fixin's an' finery, you didn't see no good chawin' tobacco layin' round loose, did you? Thanky! thanky, child! Now I looks good at you, you ain't so much changed sence de times Marse John used to wallop you for your tricks. Well, good-bye, Marse Beau."

On the leaf were scrawled the words:

"All's up! Lee has surrendered.—BEAU."

The Battleground

Elsie Singmaster

MERCIFULLY, MARY BOWMAN, a widow, whose husband had been missing since the battle of Gettysburg, had been warned, together with other citizens of Gettysburg, that on Thursday the nineteenth of November, 1863, she would be awakened from sleep by a bugler's reveillé, and that during that great day she would hear again the dread sound of cannon.

Nevertheless, hearing again the reveillé, she sat up in bed with a scream and put her hands over her ears. Then, gasping, groping about in her confusion and terror, she rose and began to dress. She put on a dress which had been once a bright plaid, but which now, having lost both its color and the stiff, outstanding quality of the skirts of '63, hung about her in straight and dingy folds. It was clean, but it had upon it certain ineradicable brown stains on which soap and water seemed to have no effect. She was thin and pale, and her eyes had a set look, as though they saw other sights than those directly about her.

In the bed from which she had risen lay her little daughter; in a trundle bed near by, her two sons, one about ten years old, the other about four. They slept heavily, lying deep in their beds, as though they would never move. Their mother looked at them with her strange, absent gaze; then she barred a little more closely the broken shutters, and went down the stairs. The shutters were broken in a curious fashion. Here and there they were pierced by round holes, and one hung from a single hinge. The window frames were without glass, the floor was without carpet, the bed without pillows.

In her kitchen Mary Bowman looked about her as though still seeing other sights. Here, too, the floor was carpetless. Above the stove a patch of fresh plaster on the wall showed where a great rent had been filled in; in the doors were the same little round holes as in the shutters of the room above. But there was food and fuel, which was more than one might have expected from the aspect of the house and its mistress. She opened the shattered door of the cupboard, and, having made the fire, began to prepare breakfast.

Outside the house there was already, at six o'clock, noise and confusion. Last evening a train from Washington had brought to the village Abraham Lincoln; for several days other trains had been bringing less distinguished guests, until thousands thronged the little town. This morning the tract of land between Mary Bowman's house and the village cemetery was to be dedicated for the burial of the Union dead, who were to be laid there in sweeping semi-circles round a center on which a great monument was to rise.

But of the dedication, of the President of the United States, of his distinguished associates, of the great crowds, of the soldiers, of the crape-banded banners, Mary Bowman and her children would see nothing. Mary Bowman would sit in her little wrecked kitchen with her children. For to her the President of the United States and others in high places who prosecuted war or who tolerated war, who called for young men to fight, were hateful. To Mary Bowman the crowds of curious persons who coveted a sight of the great battlefields were ghouls; their eyes wished to gloat upon ruin, upon fragments of the weapons of war, upon torn bits of the habiliments of soldiers; their feet longed to sink into the loose ground of hastily made graves; the discovery of a partially covered body was precious to them.

Mary Bowman knew that field! From Culp's Hill to the McPherson farm, from Big Round Top to the poorhouse, she had traveled it, searching, searching, with frantic, insane disregard of positions or of possibility. Her husband could not have fallen here among the Eleventh

Corps, he could not lie here among the unburied dead of the Louisiana Tigers! If he was in the battle at all, it was at the Angle that he fell.

She had not been able to begin her search immediately after the battle because there were forty wounded men in her little house; she could not prosecute it with diligence even later, when the soldiers had been carried to the hospitals, in the Presbyterian Church, the Catholic Church, the two Lutheran churches, the Seminary, the College, the Courthouse, and the great tented hospital on the York road. Nurses were here, Sisters of Mercy were here, compassionate women were here by the score; but still she was needed, with all the other women of the village, to nurse, to bandage, to comfort, to pray with those who must die. Little Mary Bowman had assisted at the amputation of limbs, she had helped to control strong men torn by the frenzy of delirium, she had tended poor bodies which had almost lost all semblance to humanity. Neither she nor any of the other women of the villages counted themselves especially heroic; the delicate wife of the judge, the petted daughter of the doctor, the gently bred wife of the preacher forgot that fainting at the sight of blood was one of the distinguishing qualities of their sex; they turned back their sleeves and repressed their tears, and shoulder to shoulder with Mary Bowman and her Irish neighbor, Hannah Casey, they fed the hungry and healed the sick and clothed the naked. If Mary Bowman had been herself, she might have laughed at the sight of her dresses cobbled into trousers, her skirts wrapped round the shoulders of sick men. But neither then nor ever after did Mary laugh at any incident of that summer.

Hannah Casey laughed, and by and by she began to boast. Meade, Hancock, Slocum, were noncombatants beside her. She had fought whole companies of Confederates, she had wielded bayonets, she had assisted at the spiking of a gun, she was Barbara Frietchie and Molly Pitcher combined. But all her lunacy could not make Mary Bowman smile.

Of John Bowman no trace could be found. No one could tell her anything about him, to her frantic letters no one responded. Her old friend, the village judge, wrote letters also, but could get no reply. Her husband was missing; it was probable that he lay somewhere upon this field, the field upon which they had wandered as lovers.

In midsummer a few trenches were opened, and Mary, unknown to her friends, saw them opened. At the uncovering of the first great pit, she actually helped with her own hands. For those of this generation who know nothing of war, that fact may be written down, to be passed over lightly. The soldiers, having been on other battle-fields, accepted her presence without comment. She did not cry, she only helped doggedly, and looked at what they found. That, too, may be written down for a generation which has not known war.

Immediately, an order went forth that no graves, large or small, were to be opened before cold weather. The citizens were panic-stricken with fear of an epidemic; already there were many cases of dysentery and typhoid. Now that the necessity for daily work for the wounded was past, the village became nervous, excited, irritable. Several men and boys were killed while trying to open unexploded shells; their deaths added to the general horror. There were constant visitors who sought husbands, brothers, sweethearts; with these the Gettysburg women were still able to weep, for them they were still able to care; but the constant demand for entertainment for the curious annoyed those who wished to be left alone to recover from the shock of battle. Gettysburg was prostrate, bereft of many of its worldly possessions, drained to the bottom of its well of sympathy. Its schools must be opened, its poor must be helped. Cold weather was coming and there were many, like Mary Bowman, who owned no longer any quilts or blankets, who had given away their clothes, their linen, even the precious sheets which their grandmothers had spun. Gettysburg grudged nothing, wished nothing back, it asked only to be left in peace.

When the order was given to postpone the opening of graves till fall, Mary began to go about the battle-field searching alone. Her good, obedient children stayed at home in the house or in the little field. They were beginning to grow thin and wan, they were shivering in the hot August weather, but their mother did not see. She gave them a great deal more to eat than she had herself, and they had far better clothes than her blood-stained motley.

She went about the battle-field with her eyes on the ground, her feet treading gently, anticipating loose soil or some sudden obstacle. Sometimes she stooped suddenly. To fragments of shells, to bits of blue or gray cloth, to cartridge belts or broken muskets, she paid no heed; at sight of pitiful bits of human bodies she shuddered. But there lay also upon that field little pocket Testaments, letters, trinkets, photographs. John had had her photograph and the children's, and surely he must have had some of the letters she had written!

But poor Mary found nothing.

One morning, late in August, she sat beside her kitchen table with her head on her arm. The first of the scarlet gum leaves had begun to drift down from the shattered trees; it would not be long before the ground would be covered, and those depressed spots, those tiny wooden headstones, those fragments of blue and gray be hidden. The thought smothered her. She did not cry, she had not cried at all. Her soul seemed hardened, stiff, like the terrible wounds for which she had helped to care.

Suddenly, hearing a sound, Mary had looked up. The judge stood in the doorway; he had known all about her since she was a little girl; something in his face told her that he knew also of her terrible search. She could not ask him to sit down, she said nothing at all. She had been a loquacious person, she had become an abnormally silent one. Speech hurt her.

The judge looked round the little kitchen. The rent in the wall was still unmended, the chairs were broken; there was nothing else to be seen but the table and the rusty stove and the thin, friendless-looking children standing by the door. It was the house not only of poverty and woe, but of neglect.

"Mary," said the judge, "how do you mean to live?"

Mary's thin, sunburned hand stirred a little as it lay on the table. "I do not know."

"You have these children to feed and clothe and you must furnish your house again. Mary—" The judge hesitated for a moment. John Bowman had been a schoolteacher, a thrifty, ambitious soul, who would have thought it a disgrace for his wife to earn her living. The judge laid his hand on the thin hand beside him. "Your children must have food, Mary. Come down to my house, and my wife will give you work. Come now."

Slowly Mary had risen from her chair, and smoothed down her dress and obeyed him. Down the street they went together, seeing fences still prone, seeing walls torn by shells, past the houses where the shock of battle had hastened the deaths of old persons and little children, and had disappointed the hearts of those who longed for a child, to the judge's house in the square. There wagons stood about, loaded with wheels of cannon, fragments of burst caissons, or with long, narrow pine boxes, brought from the railroad, to be stored against the day of exhumation. Men were laughing and shouting to one another, the driver of the wagon on which the long boxes were piled cracked his whip as he urged his horses.

Hannah Casey congratulated her neighbor heartily upon her finding work.

"That'll fix you up," she assured her.

She visited Mary constantly, she reported to her the news of the war, she talked at length of the coming of the President.

"I'm going to see him," she announced. "I'm going to shake him by the hand. I'm going to say, 'Hello, Abe, you old rail splitter, God bless you!' Then the bands'll play, and the people will march, and the Johnny Rebs will hear 'em in their graves."

Mary Bowman put her hands over her ears.

"I believe in my soul you'd let 'em all rise from the dead!"

"I would!" said Mary Bowman hoarsely. "I would!"

"Well, not so Hannah Casey! Look at me garden tore to bits! Look at me beds, stripped to the ropes!"

And Hannah Casey departed to her house.

Details of the coming celebration penetrated to the ears of Mary Bowman whether she wished it or not, and the gathering crowds made themselves known. They stood upon her porch, they examined the broken shutters, they wished to question her. But Mary Bowman would answer no questions, would not let herself be seen. To her the thing was horrible. She saw the battling hosts, she heard once more the roar of artillery, she smelled the smoke of battle, she was torn by its confusion. Besides, she seemed to feel in the ground beneath her a feebly stirring, suffering, ghastly host. They had begun again to open the trenches, and she looked into them.

Now, on the morning of Thursday, the nineteenth of November, her children dressed themselves and came down the steps. They had begun to have a little plumpness and color, but the dreadful light in their mother's eyes was still reflected in theirs. On the lower step they hesitated, looking at the door. Outside stood the judge, who had found time in the multiplicity of his cares, to come to the little house.

He spoke with kind but firm command.

"Mary," said he, "you must take these children to hear President Lincoln."

"What!" cried Mary.

"You must take these children to the exercises."

"I cannot!" cried Mary. "I cannot! I cannot!"

"You must!" The judge came into the room. "Let me hear no more of this going about. You are a Christian, your husband was a Christian. Do you want your children to think it is a wicked thing to die for their country? Do as I tell you, Mary."

Mary got up from her chair, and put on her children all the clothes they had, and wrapped about her own shoulders a little black coat which the judge's wife had given her. Then, as one who steps into an unfriendly sea, she started out with them into the great crowd. Once more, poor Mary said to herself, she would obey. She had seen the platform; by going round through the citizen's cemetery she could get close to it.

The November day was bright and warm, but Mary and her children shivered. Slowly she made her way close to the platform, patiently she stood and waited. Sometimes she stood with shut eyes, swaying a little. On the moonlit night of the third day of battle she had ventured from her house down toward the square to try to find some brandy for the dying men about her, and as in a dream she had seen a tall general, mounted upon a white horse with muffled hoofs, ride down the street. Bending from his saddle he had spoken, apparently to the empty air.

"Up, boys, up!"

There had risen at his command thousands of men lying asleep on pavement and street, and quietly, in an interminable line, they had stolen out like dead men toward the Seminary, to join their comrades and begin the long, long march to Hagerstown. It seemed to her that all about her dead men might rise now to look with reproach upon these strangers who disturbed their rest.

The procession was late, the orator of the day was delayed, but still Mary waited, swaying a little in her place. Presently the great guns roared forth a welcome, the bands played, the procession approached. On horseback, erect, gauntleted, the President of the United States drew rein beside the platform, and, with the orator and the other famous men, dismounted. There were great cheers, there were deep silences, there were fresh volleys of artillery, there was new music.

Of it all, Mary Bowman heard but little. Remembering the judge, whom she saw now near the President, she tried to obey the spirit as well as the letter of his command; she directed her children to look, she turned their heads toward the platform.

Men spoke and prayed and sang, and Mary stood still in her place. The orator of the day described the battle, he eulogized the dead, he proved the righteousness of this great war; his words fell upon Mary's ears unheard. If she had been asked who he was, she might have said vaguely that he was Mr. Lincoln. When he ended, she was ready to go home. There was singing; now she could slip away, through the gaps in the cemetery fence. She had done as the judge commanded and now she would go back to her house.

With her arms about her children, she started away. Then someone who stood near by took her by the hand.

"Madam," said he, "the President is going to speak!"

Half turning, Mary looked back. The thunder of applause made her shiver, made her even scream, it was so like that other thunderous sound which she would hear forever. She leaned upon her little children heavily, trying to get her breath, gasping, trying to keep her consciousness. She fixed her eyes upon the rising figure before her, she clung to the sight of him as a drowning swimmer in deep waters, she struggled to fix her thoughts upon him. Exhaustion, grief, misery threatened to engulf her, she hung upon him in desperation.

Slowly, as one who is old or tired or sick at heart, he rose to his feet, the President of the United States, the Commander in Chief of the Army and Navy, the hope of his country. Then he stood waiting. In great waves of sound the applause rose and died and rose again. He waited quietly. The winner of debate, the great champion of a great cause, the veteran in argument, the master of men, he looked down upon the throng. The clear, simple things he had to say were ready in his mind, he had thought them out, written out a first draft of them in Washington, copied it here in Gettysburg. It is probable that now, as he waited to speak, his mind traveled to other things, to the misery, the wretchedness, the slaughter of this field, to the tears of mothers, the grief of widows, the orphaning of little children.

Slowly, in his clear voice, he said what little he had to say. To the weary crowd, settling itself into position once more, the speech seemed short; to the cultivated who had been listening to the elaborate periods of great oratory, it seemed commonplace, it seemed a speech which anyone might have made. But it was not so with Mary Bowman, nor with many other unlearned persons. Mary Bowman's soul seemed to smooth itself out like a scroll, her hands lightened their clutch on her children, the beating of her heart slackened, she gasped no more.

She could not have told exactly what he said, though later she read it and learned it and taught it to her children and her children's children. She only saw him, felt him, breathed him in, this great, common, kindly man. His gaze seemed to rest upon her; it was not impossible, it was even probable, that during the hours that passed he had singled out that little group so near him, that desolate woman in her motley dress, with her children clinging about her. He said that the world would not forget this field, these martyrs; he said it in words which Mary Bowman could understand, he pointed to a future for which there was a new task.

"Daughter!" he seemed to say to her from the depths of trouble, of responsibility, of care greater than her own. "Daughter, be of good comfort!"

Unhindered now, amid the cheers, across ground which seemed no longer to stir beneath her feet, Mary Bowman went back to her house. There, opening the shutters, she bent and solemnly kissed her little children, saying to herself that henceforth they must have more than food and raiment; they must be given some joy in life.

Comrades

Elizabeth Stuart Phelps Ward

IN THE LATE May evening the soul of the summer had gone
suddenly incarnate, but the old man, indifferent and petulant, thrashed
upon his bed. He was not used to being ill, and found no consolations in
weather. Flowers regarded him observantly—one might have said criti-
cally—from the tables, the bureau, the window-sills: tulips, fleurs-de-
lis, pansies, peonies, and late lilacs, for he had a garden-loving wife who
made the most of "the dull season," after crocuses and daffodils, and
before roses. But he manifested no interest in flowers; less than usual, it
must be owned, in Patience, his wife. This was a marked incident.
They had lived together fifty years, and she had acquired her share of
the lessons of marriage, but not that ruder one given chiefly to women to
learn—she had never found herself a negligible quantity in her husband's life. She had the profound maternal instinct which is so large an
element in the love of every experienced and tender wife; and when
Reuben thrashed profanely upon his pillows, staring out of the window
above the vase of jonquils, without looking at her, clearly without thinking of her, she swallowed her surprise and tolerantly thought:

"Poor boy! To be a veteran and can't go!"

Her poor boy, being one-and-eighty, and having always had health and her, took his disappointment like a boy. He felt more outraged that he could not march with the other boys to decorate the graves to-morrow than he had been, or had felt that he was, by some of the important troubles of his long and, on the whole, comfortable life. He took it unreasonably; she could not deny that. But she went on saying, "Poor boy!" as she usually did when he was unreasonable. When he stopped thrashing and swore no more she smiled at him brilliantly. He had not said anything worse than "damn!" But he was a good Baptist, and the lapse was memorable.

"Peter?" he said. "Just h'ist the curtain a mite, won't you? I want to see across over to the shop. Has young Jabez locked up everything? Somebody's got to make sure."

Behind the carpenter's shop the lush tobacco-fields of the Connecticut valley were springing healthily. "There ain't as good a crop as there gener'lly is," the old man fretted.

"Don't you think so?" replied Patience. "Everybody says it's better. But you ought to know."

In the youth and vigor of her no woman was ever more misnamed. Patient she was not, nor gentle, nor adaptable to the teeth in the saw of life. Like wincing wood, her nature had resented it, the whole biting thing. All her gentleness was acquired, and acquired hard. She had fought like a man to endure like a woman, to accept, not to writhe and rebel. She had not learned easily how to count herself out. Something in the sentimentality or even the piety of her name had always seemed to her ridiculous; they both used to have their fun at its expense; for some years he called her Impatience, degenerating into Imp if he felt like it. When Reuben took to calling her Peter, she found it rather a relief.

"You'll have to go without me," he said, crossly.

"I'd rather stay with you," she urged. "I'm not a veteran."

"Who'd decorate Tommy then?" demanded the old man. "You wouldn't give Tommy the go-by, would you?"

"I never did—did I?" returned the wife, slowly.

"I don't know's you did," replied Reuben Oak, after some difficult reflection. Patience did not talk about Tommy. But she had lived Tommy, so she felt, all her married life, ever since she took him, the year-old baby of a year-dead first wife who had made Reuben artistically miserable. Oh, she had "lived Tommy," God knew. Her own baby had died, and there were never any more. But Tommy lived and clamored at her heart. She began by trying to be a good stepmother. In the end she did not have to try. Tommy never knew the difference; and his father had long since forgotten it. She had made him so happy that he seldom remembered anything unpleasant. He was accustomed to refer to his two conjugal partners as "my wife and the other woman."

But Tommy had the blood of a fighting father, and when the *Maine* went down, and his chance came, he, too, took it. Tommy lay dead and nameless in the trenches at San Juan. But his father had put up a tall gray slate-stone slab for him in the churchyard at home. This was close to the baby's; the baby's was little and white. So the veteran was used to "decorating Tommy" on Memorial Day. He did not trouble himself about the little white gravestone then. He had a veteran's savage jealousy of the day that was sacred to the splendid heroisms and sacrifices of the sixties.

"What do they want to go decorating all their relations for?" he argued. "Ain't there three hundred and sixty-four days in the year for *them?*"

He was militant on this point, and Patience did not contend. Sometimes she took the baby's flowers over the day after.

"If you can spare me just as well's not, I'll decorate Tommy tomorrow," she suggested, gently. "We'll see how you feel along by that."

"Tommy's got to be decorated, if I'm dead or livin'," retorted the veteran. The soldier father struggled up from his pillow, as if he would carry arms to his soldier son. Then he fell back weakly. "I wisht I had my old dog here," he complained, "my dog Tramp. I never did like a dog like that dog. But Tramp's dead, too. I don't believe them boys are coming. They've forgotten me, Peter. You haven't," he added, after some slow thought. "I don't know's you ever did, come to think."

Patience, in her blue shepherd-plaid gingham dress and white apron, was standing by the window—a handsome woman, a dozen years younger than her husband; her strong face was gentler than most strong faces are—in women. Her hair was not yet entirely white, and her lips were warm and rich. She had a round figure, not overgrown. There were times when she did not look over forty. Two or three late jonquils that had outlived their calendar in a cold spot by a wall stood on the windowsill beside her; these trembled in the slant, May afternoon light. She stroked them in their vase, as if they had been frightened or hurt. She did not immediately answer Reuben, and when she did, it was to say abruptly:

"Here's the boys! They're coming—the whole of them!—Jabez Trent, and old Mr. Succor, and David Swing on his crutches. I'll go right out 'n' let them all in."

She spoke as if they had been a phalanx. Reuben panted upon his pillows. Patience had shut the door, and it seemed to him as if it would never open. He pulled at his gray flannel dressing-gown with nervous fingers; they were carpenter's fingers—worn, but supple and intelligent. He had on his old red nightcap, and he felt the indignity, but he did not dare to take the cap off; there was too much pain underneath it.

When Patience opened the door she nodded at him girlishly. She had preceded the visitors, who followed her without speaking.

The veterans filed in slowly—three aged, disabled men. One was lame, and one was palsied; one was blind, and all were deaf.

"Here they are, Reuben," said Patience Oak. "They've all come to see you. Here's the whole Post."

Reuben's hand went to his red nightcap. He saluted gravely.

The veterans came in with dignity—David Swing, and Jabez Trent, and old Mr. Succor. David was the one on crutches, but Jabez Trent, with nodding head and swaying hand, led old Mr. Succor, who could not see.

Reuben watched them with a species of grim triumph. "I ain't blind," he thought, "and I hain't got the shakin' palsy. Nor I hain't come to crutches, either."

He welcomed his visitors with a distinctly patronizing air. He was conscious of pitying them as much as a soldier can afford to pity anything. They seemed to him very old men.

"Give 'em chairs, Peter," he commanded. "Give 'em *easy* chairs. Where's the cushions?"

"I favor a hard cheer myself," replied the blind soldier, sitting solid and straight upon the stiff bamboo chair into which he had been set down by Jabez Trent. "I'm sorry to find you so low, Reuben Oak."

"*Low!*" exploded the old soldier. "Why, nothing partikler ails me. I hain't got a thing the matter with me but a spell of rheumatics. I'll be spry as a kitten catchin' grasshoppers in a week. I can't march to-morrow—that's all. It's darned hard luck. How's your eyesight, Mr. Succor?"

145

"Some consider'ble better, sir," retorted the blind man. "I calc'late to get it back. My son's goin' to take me to a city eye-doctor. I ain't only seventy-eight. I'm too young to be blind. 'Tain't as if I was onto crutches, or I was down sick abed. How old are you, Reuben?"

"Only eighty-one!" snapped Reuben.

"He's eighty-one last March," interpolated his wife.

"He's come to a time of life when folks *do* take to their beds," returned David Swing. "Mebbe you could manage with crutches, Reuben, in a few weeks. I've been on 'em three years, since I was seventy-five. I've got to feel as if they was relations. Folks want me to ride to-morrow," he added contemptuously, "but I'll march on them crutches to decorate them graves, or I won't march at all."

Now Jabez Trent was the youngest of the veterans; he was indeed but sixty-eight. He refrained from mentioning this fact. He felt that it was indelicate to boast of it. His jerking hand moved over toward the bed, and he laid it on Reuben's with a fine gesture.

"You'll be round—you'll be round before you know it," he shouted.

"I ain't deef," interrupted Reuben, "like the rest of you." But the palsied man, hearing not at all, shouted on:

"You always had grit, Reuben, more'n most of us. You stood more, you was under fire more, you never was afraid of anything—What's rheumatics? 'Tain't Antietam."

"Nor it ain't Bull Run," rejoined Reuben. He lifted his red nightcap from his head. "Let it ache!" he said. "It ain't Gettysburg."

"It seems to me," suggested Jabez Trent, "that Reuben he's under fire just about now. *He* ain't used to bein' disabled. It appears to me he's fightin' this matter the way a soldier'd oughter. Comrades, I move he's entitled to promotion for military conduct. He'd rather than sympathy—wouldn't you, Reuben?"

"I don't feel to deserve it," muttered Reuben. "I swore to-day. Ask my wife."

"No, he didn't!" blazed Patience Oak. "He never said a thing but 'damn.' He's getting tired, though," she added, under breath. "He ain't very well." She delicately brushed the foot of Jabez Trent with the toe of her slipper.

"I guess we'd better not set any longer," observed Jabez Trent. The three veterans rose like one soldier. Reuben felt that their visit had not been what he expected. But he could not deny that he was tired out; he wondered why. He beckoned to Jabez Trent, who, shaking and coughing, bent over him.

"You'll see the boys don't forget to decorate Tommy, won't you?" he asked, eagerly. Jabez could not hear much of this, but he got the word Tommy, and nodded.

The three old men saluted silently, and when Reuben had put on his nightcap he found that they had all gone. Only Patience was in the room, standing by the jonquils, in her blue gingham dress and white apron.

"Tired?" she asked, comfortably. "I've mixed you up an egg-nog. Think you could take it?"

"They didn't stay long," complained the old man. "It don't seem to amount to much, does it?"

"You've punched your pillows all to pudding-stones," observed Patience Oak. "Let me fix 'em a little."

"I won't be fussed over!" cried Reuben, angrily. He gave one of his pillows a pettish push, and it went half across the room. Patience picked it up without remark. Reuben Oak held out a contrite hand.

"Peter, come here!" he commanded. Patience, with her maternal smile, obeyed.

"You stay, Peter, anyhow. Folks don't amount to anything. It's *you*, Peter."

Patience's eyes filled. But she hid them on the pillow beside him—he did not know why. She put up one hand and stroked his cheek.

"Just as if I was a johnnyquil," said the old man. He laughed, and grew quiet, and slept. But Patience did not move. She was afraid of waking him. She sat crouched and crooked on the edge of the bed, uncomfortable and happy.

Out on the street, between the house and the carpenter's shop, the figures of the veterans bent against the perspective of young tobacco. They walked feebly. Old Mr. Succor shook his head:

"Looks like he'd never see another Decoration Day. He's some considerable sick—an' he ain't young."

"He's got grit, though," urged Jabez Trent.

"He's pretty old," sighed David Swing. "He's consider'ble older 'n we be. He'd ought to be prepared for his summons any time at his age."

"We'll be decorating *him*, I guess, come next year," insisted old Mr.

Succor. Jabez Trent opened his mouth to say something, but he coughed too hard to speak.

"I'd like to look at Reuben's crop as we go by," remarked the blind man. "He's lucky to have the shop 'n' the crop too."

The three turned aside to the field, where old Mr. Succor appraised the immature tobacco leaves with seeing fingers.

"Connecticut's a *great* State!" he cried.

"And this here's a great town," echoed David Swing. "Look at the quota we sent—nigh a full company. And we had a great colonel," he added, proudly. "I calc'late he'd been major-general if it hadn't 'a' been for that infernal shell."

"Boys," said Jabez Trent, slowly, "Memorial Day's a great day. It's up to us to keep it that way—Boys, we're all that's left of the Charles Darlington Post."

"That's a fact," observed the blind soldier, soberly.

"That's so," said the lame one, softly.

The three did not talk any more; they walked past the tobacco-field thoughtfully. Many persons passed or met them. These recognized the veterans with marked respect, and with some perplexity. What! Only old blind Mr. Succor? Just David Swing on his crutches, and Jabez Trent with the shaking palsy? Only those poor, familiar persons whom one saw every day, and did not think much about on any other day? Heroes? These plain, obscure old men? *Heroes?*

So it befell that Patience Oak "decorated Tommy" for his father that Memorial Day. The year was 1909. The incident of which we have to tell occurred twelve months thereafter, in 1910. These, as I have gathered them, are the facts:

Time, to the old, takes an unnatural pace, and Reuben Oak felt that the year had sprinted him down the race-track of life; he was inclined to resent his eighty-second March birthday as a personal insult; but April cried over him, and May laughed at him, and he had acquired a certain grim reconciliation with the laws of fate by the time that the nation was summoned to remember its dead defenders upon their latest anniversary. This resignation was the easier because he found himself unexpectedly called upon to fill an extraordinary part in the drama and the pathos of the day.

He slept brokenly the night before, and waked early; it was scarcely five o'clock. But Patience, his wife, was already awake, lying quietly upon her pillow, with straight, still arms stretched down beside him. She was careful not to disturb him. Patience had the genius of love. She was endowed with love as a great poet is by song, or a musician by harmony, or an artist by color or form. She loved supremely, but her husband had never found it out. They were two plain people—a carpenter and his wife, plodding along the Connecticut valley industriously, with the ideals of their kind: to be true to their marriage vows, to be faithful to their children, to pay their debts. There were times when it occurred to Patience that she took more care of Reuben than Reuben did of her; but she dismissed the matter with a phrase common in her class, and covering for women most of the perplexity of married life: "You know what men are."

On the morning of which we speak, Reuben Oak had a blunt perception of the fact that it was kind in his wife to take such pains not to wake him till he got ready to begin the tremendous day before him; she always was considerate if he did not sleep well. He put down his hand and took hers with a sudden grasp, where it lay gentle and still beside him.

"Well, Peter," he said, kindly.

"Yes, dear," said Patience, instantly. "Feeling all right for to-day?"

"Fine," returned Reuben. "I don't know when I've felt so spry. I'll get right up 'n' dress."

"Would you mind staying where you are till I get your coffee heated?" asked Patience, eagerly. "You know how much stronger you always are if you wait for it. I'll have it on the heater in no time."

"I can't wait for coffee to-day," flashed Reuben. "I'm the best judge of what I need."

"Very well," said Patience, in a disappointed tone. For she had learned the final lesson of married life—not to oppose an obstinate man for his own good. But she slipped into her wrapper and made the coffee, nevertheless. When she came back with it, Reuben was lying on the bed in his flannels, with a comforter over him; he looked pale, and held out his hand impatiently for the coffee.

His feverish eyes healed as he watched her moving about the room. He thought how young and pretty her neck was when she splashed the water on it.

"Goin' to wear your black dress?" he asked. "That's right. I'm glad you are. I'll get up pretty soon."

"I'll bring you *all* your clothes," she said. "Don't you get a mite tired. I'll move up everything for you. Your uniform's all cleaned and pressed. Don't you do a thing!"

She brushed her thick hair with upraised, girlish arms, and got out her black serge dress and a white tie. He lay and watched her thoughtfully.

"Peter," he said, unexpectedly, "how long is it since we was married?"

"Forty-nine years," answered Patience, promptly. "Fifty, come next September."

"What a little creatur' you were, Peter—just a slip of a girl! And how you did take hold—Tommy and everything."

"I was 'most twenty," observed Patience, with dignity.

"You made a powerful good stepmother all the same," mused Reuben. "You did love Tommy, to beat all."

"I was fond of Tommy," answered Patience, quietly. "He was a nice little fellow."

"And then there was the baby, Patience. Pity we lost the baby! I guess you took that harder'n I did, Peter."

Patience made no reply.

"She was so dreadful young, Peter. I can't seem to remember how she looked. Can you? Pity she didn't live! You'd 'a' liked a daughter round the house, wouldn't you, Peter? Say, Peter, we've gone through a good deal, haven't we—you 'n' me? The war 'n' all that—and the two children. But there's one thing, Peter—"

Peter came over to him quietly, and sat down on the side of the bed. She was half dressed, and her still beautiful arms went around him.

"You'll tire yourself all out thinking, Reuben. You won't be able to decorate anybody if you ain't careful."

"What I was goin' to say was this," persisted Reuben. "I've always had you, Peter. And you've had me. I don't count so much, but I'm powerful fond of you, Peter. You're all I've got. Seems as if I couldn't set enough by you, somehow or nuther."

The old man hid his face upon her soft neck.

"There, there, dear!" said Patience. "Don't you think you'd better be getting dressed, Reuben? The procession's going to start pretty early. Folks are moving up and down the street. Everybody's got flowers—See?"

150

Reuben looked out of the window and over the pansy-bed with brilliant, dry eyes. His wife could see that he was keeping back the thing that he thought most about. She hurried his breakfast and brought the tray to him. He ate because she asked him to, but his hands shook. It seemed as if he clung wilfully to the old topic, escaping the new as long as he could, to ramble on.

"You've been a dreadfully amiable wife, Peter. I don't believe I could have got along with any other kind of woman."

"I didn't used to be amiable, Reuben. I wasn't born so. I used to take things hard. Don't you remember?"

But Reuben shook his head.

"No, I don't. I can't seem to think of any time you wasn't that way. Sho! How'd you get to be so, then, I'd like to know?"

"Oh, just by loving, I guess," said Patience Oak.

"We've marched along together a good while," answered the old man, brokenly.

Unexpectedly he held out his hand, and she grasped it; his was cold and weak; but hers was warm and strong. In a dull way the divination came to him—if one may speak of a dull divination—that she had always been the strength and warmth of his life. Suddenly it seemed to him a very long life. Now it was as if he forced himself to speak, as he would have charged at Fredericksburg. He felt as if he were climbing against breastworks when he said:

"I was the oldest of them all, Peter. And I was sickest, too. They all expected to come an' decorate *me* to-day." Patience nodded, without a word.

"I wouldn't of believed it, Peter; would you? Old Mr. Succor he had such good health. Who'd thought he'd tumble down the cellar stairs? If Mis' Succor'd be'n like you, Peter, he wouldn't have the chance to tumble: I never would of *thought* of David Swing's havin' pneumonia—would you, Peter? Why, in '62 he slept onto the ground in peltin', drenchin' storms an' never sneezed. He was powerful well 'n' tough, David was. And Jabez! Poor old Jabez Trent! I liked him the best of the lot, Peter. Didn't you? He was sorry for me when they come here that day an' I couldn't march along of them. . . . And now, Peter, I've got to go an' decorate *them*.

"I'm the last livin' survivor of the Charles Darlington Post," added the veteran. "I'm going to apply to the Department Commander to let me keep it up. I guess I can manage someways. *I won't be disbanded.* Let 'em disband me if they can! I'd like to see 'em do it. Peter? *Peter!*"

"I'll help you into your uniform," said Patience. "It's all brushed and nice for you."

She got him to his swaying feet, and dressed him, and the two went to the window that looked upon the flowers. The garden blurred yellow and white and purple—a dash of blood-red among the late tulips. Patience had plucked and picked for Memorial Day, she had gathered and given, and yet she could not strip her garden. She looked at it lovingly. She felt as if she stood in pansy lights and iris air.

"Peter," said the veteran, hoarsely, "they're all gone, my girl. Everybody's gone but you. You're the only comrade I've got left, Peter. . . .And, Peter, I want to tell you—I seem to understand it this morning. Peter, you're the best comrade of 'em all."

"That's worth it," said Patience, in a strange tone—"that's worth the—high cost of living."

She lifted her head. She had an exalted look. The thoughtful pansies seemed to turn their faces toward her. She felt that they understood her. Did it matter whether Reuben understood her or not? It occurred to her that it was not so important, after all, whether a man understood his wife, if he only loved her. Women fussed too much, she thought. If you loved a man you must take him as he was. Better any fate than to battle with the man you love for what he did not give, or could not give.

"I 'most wish 't you could march along of me," muttered Reuben Oak. "But you ain't a veteran."

"I don't know about that." Patience shook her head, smiling, but it was a sober smile.

"Tommy can't march," added Reuben. "He ain't here; nor he ain't in the graveyard either. There's only one other person I'd like to have go along of me. That's my old dog—my dog Tramp. That dog thought a sight of me. The United States army couldn't have kep' him away from me. But Tramp's dead. I don't know when I've thought of Tramp before. Where's he buried, Peter? Oh yes, come to think, he's under the big chestnut. Wonder we never decorated him, Peter."

"I have," confessed Patience. "I've done it quite a number of times. Reuben—Listen! I guess we've got to hurry. Seems to me I hear—"

"You hear drums," interrupted the old soldier. Suddenly he flared like light-wood on a camp-fire, and, before his wife could speak again, he had blazed out of the house.

152

The day had a certain unearthly beauty—most of our Memorial Days do have. Sometimes they scorch a little, and the processions wilt and lag. But this one, as we remember, had the climate of a happier world and the temperature of a day created for marching men—old soldiers who had left their youth and strength behind them, and who were feebler than they knew.

The Connecticut valley is not an emotional part of the map, but the town was alight with a suppressed feeling, intense, and hitherto unknown to the citizens. They were graver than they usually were on the national anniversary which had come to mean remembrance for the old and indifference for the young. There was no baseball in the village that day. The boys joined the procession soberly. The crowd was large but thoughtful. It had collected chiefly outside of the Post hall, where four old soldiers had valiantly sustained their dying organization for now two or three astonishing years.

The band was outside, below the steps; it played the "Star-Spangled Banner" and "John Brown's Body" while it waited. For some reason there was a delay in the ceremonies. It was rumored that the chaplain had not come. Then it went about that he had been summoned to a funeral, and would meet the procession at the churchyard. The chaplain was the pastor of the Congregational church. The regimental chaplain, he who used to pray for the dying boys after battle, had joined the vanished veterans long ago. The band struck up "My Country, 'tis of Thee!" The crowd began to press toward the steps of the Post hall and to sway to and fro restlessly.

Then slowly there emerged from the hall, and firmly descended the steps, the Charles Darlington Post of the Grand Army of the Republic. People held their breaths, and some sobbed. They were not all women, either.

Erect, with fiery eyes, with haughty head—shrunken in his old uniform, but carrying it proudly—one old man walked out. The crowd parted for him, and he looked neither to the right nor to the left, but he fell into the military step and began to march. In his aged arms he carried the flag of the Post. The military band preceded him, softly playing "Mine eyes have seen the glory," while the crowd formed into procession and followed him. From the whole countryside people had assembled, and the throng was considerable.

They came out into the streeet and turned toward the churchyard—the old soldier marching alone. They had begged him to ride, though the distance was small. But he had obstinately refused.

"This Post has always marched," he had replied.

Except for the military music and the sound of moving feet or wheels, the street was perfectly still. No person spoke to any other. The veteran marched with proud step. His gray head was high. Once he was seen to put the flag of his company to his lips. A little behind him the procession had instinctively fallen back and left a certain space. One could not help the feeling that this was occupied. But they who filled it, if such there had been, were invisible to the eye of the body. And the eyes of the soul are not possessed by all men.

Now the distance, as we have said, was short, and the old soldier was so exalted that it had not occurred to him that he could be fatigued. It was an astonishing sensation to him when he found himself unexpectedly faint.

Patience Oak, for some reasons of her own hardly clear to herself, did not join the procession. She chose to walk abreast of it, at the side, as near as possible, without offense to the ceremonies, to the solitary figure of her husband. She was pacing through the grass, at the edge of the sidewalk—falling as well as she could into the military step. In her plain, old-fashioned black dress, with the fleck of white at her throat, she had a statuesque, unmodern look. Her fine features were charged with that emotion which any expression would have weakened. Her arms were heaped with flowers—bouquets and baskets and sprays; spiraea, lilacs, flowering almond, peonies, pansies, all the glory of her garden that opening summer returned to her care and tenderness. She was tender with everything—a man, a child, an animal, a flower. Everything blossomed for her, and rested in her, and yearned toward her. The emotion of the day and of the hour seemed incarnate in her. She embodied in her strong and sweet personality all that blundering man has wrought on tormented woman by the savagery of war. She remembered what she had suffered—a young, incredulous creature, on the margin of life, avid of happiness, believing in joy, and drowning in her love for that one man, her husband. She thought of the slow news after slaughtering battles—how she waited for the laggard paper in the country town; she remembered that she dared not read the head-lines when she got them, but dropped, choking and praying God to spare her, before she glanced. Even now she could feel the wet paper against her raining cheek. Then her heart leaped back, and she thought of the day when he marched away—his arms, his lips, his groans. She remembered what the dregs of desolation were, and mortal fear of unknown fate; the rack of the imagination; and inquisition of the nerve—the pangs that no man-soldier of them all could understand. "It comes on women—war," she thought.

Now, as she was stepping aside to avoid crushing some young white clover-blossoms in the grass where she was walking, she looked up and wondered if she were going blind, or if her mind were giving way.

The vacant space behind the solitary veteran trembled and palpitated before her vision, as if it had been peopled. By what? By whom? Patience was no occultist. She had never seen an apparition in her life. She felt that if she had not lacked a mysterious, unknown gift, she should have seen spirits, as men marching, now. But she did not see them. She was aware of a tremulous, nebulous struggle in the empty air, as of figures that did not form, or of sights from which her eyes were holden. Ah—what? She gasped for the wonder of it. Who was it that followed the veteran, with the dumb, delighted fidelity that one race only knows, of all created? For a wild instant this sane and sensible woman could have taken oath that Reuben Oak was accompanied on his march by his old dog, his dead dog, Tramp. If it had been Tommy—Or if it had been Jabez Trent—And where were they who had gone into the throat of death with him at Antietam, at Bull Run, at Fair Oaks, at Malvern Hill? But there limped along behind Reuben only an old, forgotten dog.

This quaint delusion (if delusion we must call it) aroused her attention, which had wavered from her husband, and concentrated it upon him afresh. Suddenly she saw him stagger.

A dozen persons started, but the wife sprang and reached him first. As she did this, the ghost dog vanished from before her. Only Reuben was there, marching alone, with the unpeopled space between him and the procession.

"Leave go of me!" he gasped. Patience quietly grasped him by the arm, and fell into step beside him. In her heart she was terrified.

"I'll march to decorate the Post—and Tommy—if I drop dead for it!" panted Reuben Oak.

"Then I shall march beside you," answered Patience.

"What'll folks say?" cried the old soldier, in real anguish.

"They'll say I'm where I belong. Reuben! Reuben! I've *earned the right to.*"

He contended no more, but yielded to her—in fact, gladly, for he felt too weak to stand alone. Inspiring him, and supporting him, and yet seeming (such was the sweet womanliness of her) to lean on him, Patience marched with him before the people; and these saw her through blurred eyes, and their hearts saluted her. With every step she felt that he strengthened. She was conscious of endowing him with her own vitality.

So the veteran and his wife came on together to the cemetery, with the flags and the flowers.

In the churchyard it was pleasant and expectant. The morning was cool, and the sun climbed gently. Not a flower had wilted; they looked as if they had been planted and were growing on the graves. When they had come to these, Patience Oak held back. She would not take from the old soldier his precious right. She did not offer to help him "decorate" anybody. His trembling fingers clutched at the flowers as if he had been handling shot or nails. His breath came short.

"Hadn't you better sit down and rest?" she whispered. But he paid no attention to her, and crawled from mound to mound. She perceived that it was his will to leave the new-made graves until the others had been remembered. Then he tottered across the cemetery with the flowers that he had saved for David Swing and old Mr. Succor and Jabez Trent, and the cheeks of the Charles Darlington Post were wet. Last of all he "decorated Tommy."

As his sacred task drew to its end he grew remote, elate, and solemn. It was as if he were transfigured into something strange and holy. A village carpenter? A Connecticut tobacco-planter? Rather, say, the glory of the nation, the guardian of a great trust, proudly carried, and honored to its end.

Taps were sounding over the old graves and the new, when the veteran slowly sank to one knee and toppled over. Patience, when she got her arms about him, saw that he had fallen across the mound where he had decorated Tommy with her white lilacs. Beyond lay the baby. The wife sat down on the little grave and drew the old man's head upon her lap.

"You *shall not* die!" she said.

She gathered him and poured her powerful being upon him—breath, warmth, will, prayer, who could say what it was? She felt as if she took hold of tremendous, unseen forces and moved them by unknown powers.

The flag had fallen from his arms at last; he had clung to it till now. The chaplain reverently lifted it and laid it at his feet.

Once his white lips moved, and the people hushed to hear what outburst of patriotism would issue from them—what tribute to the cause that he had fought for, what final apostrophe to his country or his flag. "Peter?" he called, feebly. *"Peter!"*

But Peter had said he should not die. And Peter knew. Had not she always known what he should do, or what he could? He lay upon his bed peacefully when, with tears and smiles, in reverence and in wonder, they had brought him home—and the flag of the Post, too. By a gesture he had asked to have it hung upon the foot-board of his bed.

He turned his head upon his pillow and watched his wife with wide, reflecting eyes. It was a long time before she would let him talk; in fact, the May afternoon was slanting to dusk before he tried to cross her tender will about that matter. When he did, it was to say only this:

"Peter? I was goin' to decorate the baby. I meant to when I took that turn."

Peter nodded.

"It's all done, Reuben."

"And, Peter? I've had the queerest notions about my old dog Tramp to-day. I wonder if there's a johnnyquil left to decorate *him?*"

"I'll go and see," said Peter. But when she had come back he had forgotten Tramp and the johnnyquil.

"Peter," he muttered, "this has been a great day." He gazed solemnly at the flag.

Patience regarded him poignantly. With a stricture at the heart she thought:

"He has grown old fast since yesterday." Then joyously the elderly wife cried out upon herself: "But I am young! He shall have all my youth. I've got enough for two—and strength!"

She crept beside him and laid her warm cheek to his.

The Burning

Eudora Welty

DELILAH WAS DANCING up to the front with a message; that was
how she happened to be the one to see. A horse was coming in the house,
by the front door. The door had been shoved wide open. And all
behind the horse, a crowd with a long tail of dust was coming after, all
the way up their road from the gate between the cedar trees.

She ran on into the parlor, where they were. They were standing up
before the fireplace, their white sewing dropped over their feet, their
backs turned, both ladies. Miss Theo had eyes in the back of her head.

"Back you go, Delilah," she said.

"It ain't me, it's them," cried Delilah, and now there were running
feet to answer all over the downstairs; Ophelia and all had heard. Outside the dogs were thundering. Miss Theo and Miss Myra, keeping
their backs turned to whatever shape or ghost Commotion would take
when it came—as long as it was still in the yard, mounting the steps,
crossing the porch, or even, with a smell of animal sudden as the smell of
snake, planting itself in the front hall—they still had to see it if it came in
the parlor, the white horse. It drew up just over the ledge of the double
doors Delilah had pushed open, and the ladies lifted their heads together

and looked in the mirror over the fireplace, the one called the Venetian mirror, and there it was.

It was a white silhouette, like something cut out of the room's dark. July was so bright outside, and the parlor so dark for coolness, that at first nobody but Delilah could see. Then Miss Myra's racing speech interrupted everything.

"Will you take me on the horse? Please take me first."

It was a towering, sweating, grimacing, uneasy white horse. It had brought in two soldiers with red eyes and clawed, mosquito-racked faces—one a rider, hang-jawed and head-hanging, and the other walking by its side, all breathing in here now as loud as trumpets.

Miss Theo with shut eyes spoke just behind Miss Myra. "Delilah, what is it you came in your dirty apron to tell me?"

The sisters turned with linked hands and faced the room.

"Come to tell you we got the eggs away from black broody hen and sure enough, they's addled," said Delilah.

She saw the blue rider drop his jaw still lower. That was his laugh. But the other soldier set his boot on the carpet and heard the creak in the floor. As if reminded by tell-tale, he took another step, and with his red eyes sticking out he went as far as Miss Myra and took her around that little bending waist. Before he knew it, he had her lifted as high as a child, she was so light. The other soldier with a grunt came down from the horse's back and went toward Miss Theo.

"Step back, Delilah, out of harm's way," said Miss Theo, in such a company-voice that Delilah thought harm was one of two men.

"Hold my horse, nigger," said the man it was.

Delilah took the bridle as if she'd always done that, and held the horse that loomed there in the mirror—she could see it there now, herself—while more blurred and blind-like in the room between it and the door the first soldier shoved the tables and chairs out of the way behind Miss Myra, who flitted when she ran, and pushed her down where she stood and dropped on top of her. There in the mirror the parlor remained, filled up with dusted pictures, and shuttered since six o'clock against the heat and that smell of smoke they were all so tired of, still glimmering with precious, breakable things white ladies were never tired of and never broke, unless they were mad at each other. Behind *her*, the bare yawn of the hall was at her back, and the front stair's shadow, big as a tree and empty. Nobody went up there without being seen, and nobody was supposed to come down. Only if a cup or a silver spoon or a little string of spools on a blue ribbon came hopping down the steps like a frog, sometimes Delilah was the one to pick it up and run back up with it. Outside the mirror's frame, the flat of Miss Theo's hand came down on mankind with a boisterous sound.

Then Miss Theo lifted Miss Myra without speaking to her; Miss Myra closed her eyes but was not asleep. Her bands of black hair awry, her clothes rustling stiffly as clothes through winter quiet, Miss Theo strode half-carrying Miss Myra to the chair in the mirror, and put her down. It was the red, rubbed velvet, pretty chair like Miss Myra's ringbox. Miss Myra threw her head back, face up to the little plaster flowers going around the ceiling. She was asleep somewhere, if not in her eyes.

One of the men's voices spoke out, all gone with righteousness. "We just come in to inspect."

"You presume, you dare," said Miss Theo. Her hand came down to stroke Miss Myra's back-flung head in a strong, forbidding rhythm. From upstairs, Phinny threw down his breakfast plate, but Delilah did not move. Miss Myra's hair streamed loose behind her, bright gold, with the combs caught like leaves in it. Maybe it was to keep her like this, asleep in the heart, that Miss Theo stroked her on and on, too hard.

"It's orders to inspect beforehand," said the soldier.

"Then inspect," said Miss Theo. "No one in the house to prevent it. Brother—no word. Father—dead. Mercifully so—" She spoke in an almost rough-and-tumble kind of way used by ladies who didn't like company—never did like company, for anybody.

Phinny threw down his cup. The horse, shivering, nudged Delilah who was holding him there, a good obedient slave in her fresh-ironed candy-stripe dress beneath her black apron. She would have had her turban tied on, had she known all this ahead, like Miss Theo. "Never is Phinny away. Phinny here. He a he," she said.

Miss Myra's face was turned up as if she were dead, or as if she were a fierce and hungry little bird. Miss Theo rested her hand for a moment in the air above her head.

"Is it shame that's stopping your inspection?" Miss Theo asked. "I'm afraid you found the ladies of this house a trifle out of your element. My sister's the more delicate one, as you see. May I offer you this young kitchen Negro, as I've always understood—"

That Northerner gave Miss Theo a serious, recording look as though she had given away what day the mail came in.

"My poor little sister," Miss Theo went on to Miss Myra, "don't mind what you hear. Don't mind this old world." But Miss Myra knocked back the stroking hand. Kitty came picking her way into the room and sat between the horse's front feet; Friendly was her name.

One soldier rolled his head toward the other. "What was you saying to me when we come in, Virge?"

"I was saying I opined they wasn't gone yet."

"*Warn't* they?"

Suddenly both of them laughed, jolting each other so hard that for a second it looked like a fight. Then one said with straight face, "We come with orders to set the house afire, ma'am," and the other one said, "General Sherman."

"I hear you."

"Don't you think we're going to do it? We done just burnt up Jackson twice," said the first soldier with his eye on Miss Myra. His voice made a man's big echo in the hall, like a long time ago. The horse whinnied and moved his head and feet.

"Like I was telling you, you ladies ought to been out. You didn't get no word here we was coming?" The other soldier pointed one finger at Miss Theo. She shut her eyes.

"Lady, they told you." Miss Myra's soldier looked hard at Miss Myra there. "And when your own people tell you something's coming to burn your house down, the business-like thing to do is get out of the way. And the right thing. I ain't beholden to tell you no more times now."

"Then go."

"Burning up *people's* further'n I go yet."

Miss Theo stared him down. "I see no degree."

So it was Miss Myra's soldier that jerked Delilah's hand from the bridle and turned her around, and cursed the Bedlam-like horse which began to beat the hall floor behind. Delilah listened, but Phinny did not throw anything more down; maybe he had crept to the landing, and now looked over. He was scared, if not of horses, then of men. He didn't know anything about them. The horse did get loose; he took a clattering trip through the hall and dining room and library, until at last his rider caught him. Then Delilah was set on his back.

She looked back over her shoulder through the doorway, and saw Miss Theo shake Miss Myra and catch the peaked face with its purple eyes and slap it.

"Myra," she said, "collect your senses. We have to go out in front of them."

Miss Myra slowly lifted her white arm, like a lady who has been asked to dance, and called, "Delilah!" Because that was the one she saw being lifted onto the horse's hilly back and ridden off through the front door. Skittering among the iron shoes, Kitty came after, trotting fast as a little horse herself, and ran ahead to the woods, where she was never seen again; but Delilah, from where she was set up on the horse and then dragged down on the grass, never called after her.

She might have been saving her breath for the screams that soon took over the outdoors and circled that house they were going to finish for sure now. She screamed, young and strong, for them all—for everybody that wanted her to scream for them, for everybody that didn't; and sometimes it seemed to her that she was screaming her loudest for Delilah, who was lost now—carried out of the house, not knowing how to get back.

Still inside, the ladies kept them waiting.

Miss Theo finally brought Miss Myra out through that wide-open front door and across the porch with the still perfect and motionless vine shadows. There were some catcalls and owl hoots from under the trees.

"Now hold back, boys. They's too ladylike for you."

"Ladies must needs take their time."

"And then they're no damn good at it!" came a clear, youthful voice, and under the branches somewhere a banjo was stroked to call up the campfires further on, later in the evening, when all this would be over and done.

The sisters showed no surprise to see soldiers and Negroes alike (old Ophelia in the way, talking, talking) strike into and out of the doors of the house, the front now the same as the back, to carry off beds, tables, candlesticks, washstands, cedar buckets, china pitchers, with their backs bent double; or the horses ready to go; or the food of the kitchen bolted down—and so much of it thrown away, this must be a second dinner; or the unsilenceable dogs, the old pack mixed with the strangers and fighting with all their hearts over bones. The last skinny sacks were thrown on the wagons—the last flour, the last scraping and clearing from Ophelia's shelves, even her pepper-grinder. The silver Delilah could count was counted on strange blankets and then, knocking against the teapot, rolled together, tied up like a bag of bones. A drummer boy with his drum around his neck caught both Miss Theo's peacocks, Marco and Polo, and wrung their necks in the yard. Nobody could look at those bird-corpses; nobody did.

The sisters left the porch like one, and in step, hands linked, came through the high grass in their crushed and only dresses, and walked under the trees. They came to a stop as if it was moonlight under the leafy frame of the big tree with the swing, without any despising left in their faces which were the same as one, as one face that didn't belong to anybody. This one clarified face, looking both left and right, could make out every one of those men through the bushes and tree trunks, and mark every looting slave also, as all stood momently fixed like serenaders by the light of a moon. Only old Ophelia was talking all the time, all the time, telling everybody in her own way about the trouble here, but of course nobody could understand a thing that day anywhere in the world.

"What are they fixing to do now, Theo?" asked Miss Myra, with a frown about to burn into her too-white forehead.

"What they want to," Miss Theo said, folding her arms.

To Delilah that house they were carrying the torches to was like one just now coming into being—like the showboat that slowly came through the trees just once in her time, at the peak of high water—bursting with the unknown, sparking in ruddy light, with a minute to go before that ear-aching cry of the calliope.

When it came—but it was a bellowing like a bull, that came from inside—Delilah drew close, with Miss Theo's skirt to peep around, and Miss Theo's face looked down like death itself and said, "Remember this. You black monkeys," as the blaze outdid them all.

A while after the burning, when everybody had gone away, Miss Theo and Miss Myra, finding and taking hold of Delilah, who was face-down in a ditch with her eyes scorched open, did at last go beyond the tramped-down gate and away through the grand worthless fields they themselves had burned long before.

It was a hot afternoon, hot out here in the open, and it played a trick on them with a smell and prophecy of fall—it was the burning. The brown wet standing among the stumps in the cracked cup of the pond tasted as hot as coffee and as bitter. There was still and always smoke between them and the sun.

After all the July miles, there Jackson stood, burned twice, or who knew if it was a hundred times, facing them in the road. Delilah could see through Jackson like a haunt, it was all chimneys, all scooped out. There were soldiers with guns among the ashes, but these ashes were cold. Soon even these two ladies, who had been everywhere and once knew their way, told each other they were lost. While some soldiers looked them over, they pointed at what they couldn't see, traced gone-away spires, while a horse without his rider passed brushing his side against them and ran down a black alley softly, and did not return.

They walked here and there, sometimes over the same track, holding hands all three, like the timeless time it snowed, and white and black went to play together in hushed woods. They turned loose only to point and name.

"The State House."—"The school."

"The Blind School."—"The penitentiary!"

"The big stable."—"The Deaf-and-Dumb."

"Oh! Remember when we passed three of *them*, sitting on a hill?" They went on matching each other, naming and claiming ruin for ruin.

"The lunatic asylum!"—"The State House."

"No, I said that. Now where are we? That's surely Captain Jack Calloway's hitching post."

"But why would the hitching post be standing and the rest not?"

"And ours not."

"I think I should have told you, Myra—"

"Tell me now."

"Word *was* sent to us to get out when it was sent to the rest on Vicksburg Road. Two days' warning. I believe it was a message from General Pemberton."

"Don't worry about it now. Oh no, of course we couldn't leave," said Miss Myra. A soldier watched her in the distance, and she recited:

"There was a man in our town
And he was wondrous wise.
He jumped into a bramble bush
And scratched out both his eyes."

She stopped, looking at the soldier.

"He sent word," Miss Theo went on, "General Pemberton sent word, for us all to get out ahead of what was coming. You were in the summerhouse when it came. It was two days' warning—but I couldn't bring myself to call and tell you, Myra. I suppose I couldn't convince myself—couldn't quite *believe* that they meant to come and visit that destruction on us."

"Poor Theo. I could have."

"No you couldn't. I couldn't *understand* that message, any more than Delilah here could have. I can reproach myself now, of course, with everything." And they began to walk boldly through and boldly out of the burnt town, single file.

"Not everything, Theo. Who had Phinny? Remember?" cried Miss Myra ardently.

"Hush."

"If I hadn't had Phinny, that would've made it all right. Then Phinny wouldn't have—"

"Hush, dearest, that wasn't *your* baby, you know. It was Brother Benton's baby. I won't have your nonsense now." Miss Theo led the way through the ashes, marching in front. Delilah was in danger of getting left behind.

"—perished. Dear Benton. So good. Nobody else would have felt so *bound*," Miss Myra said.

"Not after I told him what he owed a little life! Each little life is a *man's* fault. Oh, who'll ever forget that awful day?"

"Benton's forgotten, if he's dead. He was so good after that too, never married."

"Stayed home, took care of his sisters. Only wanted to be forgiven."

"There has to be somebody to take care of everybody."

"I told him, he must never dream he was *inflicting* his sisters. That's what we're for."

"And it never would have inflicted us. We could have lived and died. Until *they* came."

"In at the front door on the back of a horse," said Miss Theo. "If Benton had been there!"

"I'll never know what possessed them, riding in like that," said Miss Myra almost mischievously; and Miss Theo turned.

"And *you said*—"

"I said something wrong," said Miss Myra quickly. "I apologize, Theo."

"No, I blame only myself. That I let you remain one hour in that house after it was doomed. I thought I was equal to it, and I proved I was, but not you."

"Oh, to my shame you saw me, dear! Why do you say it wasn't my baby?"

"Now don't start that nonsense over again," said Miss Theo, going around a hole.

"I had Phinny. When we were all at home and happy together. Are you going to take Phinny away from me now?"

Miss Theo pressed her cheeks with her palms and showed her pressed, pensive smile as she looked back over her shoulder.

Miss Myra said, "Oh, don't *I* know who it really belonged to, who it loved the best, that baby?"

"I won't have you misrepresenting yourself."

"It's never what I intended."

"Then reason dictates you hush."

Both ladies sighed, and so did Delilah; they were tired of going on. Miss Theo still walked in front but she was looking behind her through the eyes in the back of her head.

"You hide him if you want to," said Miss Myra. "Let Papa shut up all upstairs. I had him, dear. It was an officer, no, one of our beaux that used to come out and hunt with Benton. It's because I was always the impetuous one, highstrung and so easily carried away...And if Phinny *was* mine—"

"Don't you know he's black?" Miss Theo blocked the path.

"He *was* white." Then, "He's black *now*," whispered Miss Myra, darting forward and taking her sister's hands. Their shoulders were pressed together, as if they were laughing or waiting for something more to fall.

"If I only had something to eat!" sobbed Miss Myra, and once more let herself be embraced. One eye showed over the tall shoulder. "Oh, Delilah!"

"Could be he got out," called Delilah in a high voice. "He strong, he."

"Who?"

"Could be Phinny's out loose. Don't cry."

"Look yonder. What do I see? I see the Dicksons' perfectly good hammock still under the old pecan trees," Miss Theo said to Miss Myra, and spread her hand.

There was some little round silver cup, familiar to the ladies, in the hammock when they came to it down in the grove. Lying on its side with a few drops in it, it made them smile.

The yard was charged with butterflies. Miss Myra, as if she could wait no longer, climbed into the hammock and lay down with ankles crossed. She took up the cup like a story book she'd begun and left there yesterday, holding it before her eyes in those freckling fingers, slowly picking out the ants.

"So still out here and all," Miss Myra said. "Such a big sky. Can you get used to that? And all the figs dried up. I wish it would rain."

"Won't rain till Saturday," said Delilah.

"Delilah, don't go 'way."

"Don't you try, Delilah," said Miss Theo.

"No'm."

Miss Theo sat down, rested a while, though she did not know how to sit on the ground and was afraid of grasshoppers, and then she stood up, shook out her skirt, and cried out to Delilah, who had backed off far to one side, where some chickens were running around loose with nobody to catch them.

"Come back here, Delilah! Too late for that!" She said to Miss Myra, "The Lord will provide. We've still got Delilah, and as long as we've got her we'll use her, my dearie."

Miss Myra "let the cat die" in the hammock. Then she gave her hand to climb out, Miss Theo helped her, and without needing any help for herself Miss Theo untied the hammock from the pecan trees. She was long bent over it, and Miss Myra studied the butterflies. She had left the cup sitting on the ground in the shade of the tree. At last Miss Theo held up two lengths of cotton rope, the red and the white strands untwisted from each other, bent like the hair of ladies taken out of plaits in the morning.

Delilah, given the signal, darted up the tree and hooking her toes made the ropes fast to the two branches a sociable distance apart, where Miss Theo pointed. When she slid down, she stood waiting while they settled it, until Miss Myra repeated enough times, in a spoiled sweet way, "I bid to be first." It was what Miss Theo wanted all the time.

Then Delilah had to squat and make a basket with her fingers, and Miss Myra tucked up her skirts and stepped her ashy shoe in the black hands.

"Tuck under, Delilah."

Miss Myra, who had ordered that, stepped over Delilah's head and stood on her back, and Delilah felt her presence tugging there as intimately as a fish's on a line, each longing Miss Myra had to draw away from Miss Theo, draw away from Delilah, away from that tree.

Delilah rolled her eyes around. The noose was being tied by Miss Theo's puckered hands like a bonnet on a windy day, and Miss Myra's young lifted face was looking out.

"I learned as a child how to tie, from a picture book in Papa's library—not that I ever was called on," Miss Theo said. "I guess I was always something of a tomboy." She kissed Miss Myra's hand and at almost the same instant Delilah was seized by the ribs and dragged giggling backward, out from under—not soon enough, for Miss Myra kicked her in the head—a bad kick, almost as if that were Miss Theo or a man up in the tree, who meant what he was doing.

Miss Theo stood holding Delilah and looking up—helping herself to grief. No wonder Miss Myra used to hide in the summerhouse with her reading, screaming sometimes when there was nothing but Delilah throwing the dishwater out on the ground.

"I've proved," said Miss Theo to Delilah, dragging her by more than main force back to the tree, "what I've always suspicioned: that I'm brave as a lion. That's right: look at me. If I ordered you back up that tree to help my sister down to the grass and shade, you'd turn and run: I know your minds. You'd desert me with your work half done. So I haven't said a word about it. About mercy. As soon as you're through, you can go, and leave us where you've put us, unspared, just alike. And that's the way they'll find us. The sight will be good for them for what they've done," and she pushed Delilah down and walked up on her shoulders, weighting her down like a rock.

Miss Theo looped her own knot up there; there was no mirror or sister to guide her. Yet she was quicker this time than last time, but Delilah was quicker too. She rolled over in a ball, and then she was up running, looking backward, crying. Behind her Miss Theo came sailing down from the tree. She was always too powerful for a lady. Even those hens went flying up with a shriek, as if they felt her shadow on their backs. Now she reached in the grass.

There was nothing for Delilah to do but hide, down in the jungly grass choked with bitterweed and black-eyed susans, wild to the pricking skin, with many heads nodding, cauldrons of ants, with butterflies riding them, grasshoppers hopping them, mosquitoes making the air alive, down in the loud and lonesome grass that was rank enough almost to matt the sky over. Once, stung all over and wild to her hair's ends, she ran back and asked Miss Theo, "What must I do now? Where must I go?" But Miss Theo, whose eyes from the ground were looking straight up at her, wouldn't tell. Delilah danced away from her, back to her distance, and crouched down. She believed Miss Theo twisted in the grass like a dead snake until the sun went down. She herself held still like a mantis until the grass had folded and spread apart at the falling of dew. This was after the chickens had gone to roost in a strange uneasy tree against the cloud where the guns still boomed and the way from Vicksburg was red. Then Delilah could find her feet.

She knew where Miss Theo was. She could see the last white of Miss Myra, the stockings. Later, down by the swamp, in a wading bird tucked in its wing for sleep, she saw Miss Myra's ghost.

After being lost a day and a night or more, crouching awhile, stealing awhile through the solitudes of briar bushes, she came again to Rose Hill. She knew it by the chimneys and by the crape myrtle off to the side, where the bottom of the summerhouse stood empty as an egg basket. Some of the flowers looked tasty, like chicken legs fried a little black.

Going around the house, climbing over the barrier of the stepless back doorsill, and wading into ashes, she was lost still, inside that house. She found an iron pot and a man's long boot, a doorknob and a little book fluttering, its leaves spotted and fluffed like guinea feathers. She took up the book and read out from it, "Ba-ba-ba-ba-ba—trash." She was being Miss Theo taking away Miss Myra's reading. Then she saw the Venetian mirror down in the chimney's craw, flat and face-up in the cinders.

Behind her the one standing wall of the house held notched and listening like the big ear of King Solomon into which poured the repeated asking of birds. The tree stood and flowered. What must she do? Crouching suddenly to the ground, she heard the solid cannon, the galloping, the low fast drum of burning. Crawling on her knees she went to the glass and rubbed it with spit and leaned over it and saw a face all neck and ears, then gone. Before it she opened and spread her arms; she had seen Miss Myra do that, try that. But its gleam was addled.

Though the mirror did not know Delilah, Delilah would have known that mirror anywhere, because it was set between black men. Their arms were raised to hold up the mirror's roof, which now the swollen mirror brimmed, among gold leaves and gold heads—black men dressed in gold, looking almost into the glass themselves, as if to look back through a door, men now half-split away, flattened with fire, bearded, noseless as the moss that hung from swamp trees.

Where the mirror did not cloud like the horse-trampled spring, gold gathered itself from the winding water, and honey under water started to flow, and then the gold fields were there, hardening gold. Through the water, gold and honey twisted up into houses, trembling. She saw people walking the bridges in early light with hives of houses on their heads, men in dresses, some with red birds; and monkeys in velvet; and ladies with masks laid over their faces looking from pointed windows. Delilah supposed that was Jackson before Sherman came. Then it was gone. In this noon quiet, here where all had passed by, unless indeed it had gone in, she waited on her knees.

The mirror's cloudy bottom sent up minnows of light to the brim where now a face pure as a water-lily shadow was floating. Almost too small and deep down to see, they were quivering, leaping to life, fighting, aping old things Delilah had seen done in this world already, sometimes what men had done to Miss Theo and Miss Myra and the peacocks and to slaves, and sometimes what a slave had done and what anybody now could do to anybody. Under the flicker of the sun's licks, then under its whole blow and blare, like an unheard scream, like an act of mercy gone, as the wall-less light and July blaze struck through from the opened sky, the mirror felled her flat.

She put her arms over her head and waited, for they would all be coming again, gathering under her and above her, bees saddled like horses out of the air, butterflies harnessed to one another, bats with masks on, birds together, all with their weapons bared. She listened for the blows, and dreaded that whole army of wings—of flies, birds, serpents, their glowing enemy faces and bright kings' dresses, that banner of colors forked out, all this world that was flying, striking, stricken, falling, gilded or blackened, mortally splitting and falling apart, proud turbans unwinding, turning like the spotted dying leaves of fall, spiraling down to bottomless ash; she dreaded the fury of all the butterflies and dragonflies in the world riding, blades unconcealed and at point—descending, and rising again from the waters below, down under, one whale made of his own grave, opening his mouth to swallow Jonah one more time.

Jonah!—a homely face to her, that could still look back from the red lane he'd gone down, even if it was too late to speak. He was her Jonah, her Phinny, her black monkey; she worshiped him still, though it was long ago he was taken from her the first time.

Stiffly, Delilah got to her feet. She cocked her head, looked sharp into the mirror, and caught the motherly image—head wagging in the flayed forehead of a horse with ears and crest up stiff, the shield and the drum of big swamp birdskins, the horns of deer sharpened to cut and kill with. She showed her teeth. Then she looked in the feathery ashes and found Phinny's bones. She ripped a square from her manifold fullness of skirts and tied up the bones in it.

She set foot in the road then, walking stilted in Miss Myra's shoes and carrying Miss Theo's shoes tied together around her neck, her train in the road behind her. She wore Miss Myra's willing rings—had filled up two fingers—but she had had at last to give up the puzzle of Miss Theo's bracelet with the chain. They were two stones now, scalding-white. When the combs were being lifted from her hair, Miss Myra had come down too, beside her sister.

Light on Delilah's head the Jubilee cup was set. She paused now and then to lick the rim and taste again the ghost of sweet that could still make her tongue start clinging—some sweet lapped up greedily long ago, only a mystery now when or who by. She carried her own black locust stick to drive the snakes.

Following the smell of horses and fire, to men, she kept in the wheel tracks till they broke down at the river. In the shade underneath the burned and fallen bridge she sat on a stump and chewed for a while, without dreams, the comb of a dirtdauber. Then once more kneeling, she took a drink from the Big Black, and pulled the shoes off her feet and waded in.

Submerged to the waist, to the breast, stretching her throat like a sunflower stalk above the river's opaque skin, she kept on, her treasure stacked on the roof of her head, hands laced upon it. She had forgotten how or when she knew, and she did not know what day this was, but she knew—it would not rain, the river would not rise, until Saturday.

LOUISA MAY ALCOTT (1832-1888) was born in Germantown, Pennsylvania, and lived in Concord, Massachusetts. She turned to writing to support herself and her family after the utopian schemes of her father, Bronson Alcott, had failed. Best known for her novels for young people—*Little Women, Little Men, Eight Cousins, Rose in Bloom*, and others—she wrote lesser-known works in several genres. *Hospital Sketches* (1863) was based on her experiences as a Civil War field nurse.

KATE CHOPIN (1851-1904), who was part French Creole and part Irish, was born Katherine O'Flaherty in St. Louis and was educated at the Sacred Heart Convent there. With her husband, Oscar Chopin, she moved to New Orleans, and a few years later to Cloutierville, Louisiana, in Natchitoches Parish. Her short stories were collected in *Bayou Folk* (1894) and *A Night in Acadie* (1897). Her last novel, *The Awakening* (1899), is highly regarded as a precursor of modernist and feminist writing.

ROSE TERRY COOKE (1827-1892) was born in Hartford, Connecticut, to an old New England family. After attending the Hartford Female Seminary she taught school, until an inheritance allowed her to turn to full-time writing. She published more than 100 short stories in respected journals of her day. "A Woman" first appeared in the *Atlantic Monthly* (December 1862).

CAROLINE GORDON (1895-1981) grew up in Kentucky and received her B.A. in 1916 from Bethany College in West Virginia. After teaching high school, she became a journalist for the *Chattanooga News*. Other important points in her life were her marriage to Allen Tate in 1924 and her conversion to Catholicism in 1947. Her novels include *Penhally* (1931), *The Strange Children* (1951), and *The Malefactors* (1956); *The Collected Stories of Caroline Gordon* was published in 1981.

ALBERTA PIERSON HANNUM (1906-   ) was born in Candit, Ohio. Her many novels include *Thursday April* (1931), *Paint the Wind* (1958), and *The Gods and One* (1941). "Turkey Hunt," first published in *Story* magazine in 1937, also appeared in *The Best Short Stories of 1938*.

GRACE KING (1851-1932), a New Orleans native, was a Presbyterian educated at a French Creole school. When she was nine, her patrician family fled occupied New Orleans to live at L'Embarrass Plantation near New Iberia, Louisiana. The family returned to New Orleans several years later with hardly anything to their name—a circumstance that may account for King's interest in social upheaval. King achieved national recognition for her fiction early in her life, though later she became known as mainly a regionalist. "Bayou l'Ombre," which was collected in *Tales of a Time and Place* (1892), first appeared in *Harper's Magazine* (July 1887).

ELSIE SINGMASTER (1879-1958), born in Schuykill Haven, Pennsylvania, was of German Lutheran and Quaker stock. She attended West Chester Normal School and Cornell and was graduated from Radcliffe in 1907. Later she won honorary degrees from several colleges. She lived at Gettysburg and wrote short stories, adult and juvenile novels, and biography. "Battleground" appeared in her collection *Gettysburg* (Houghton Mifflin, 1930, 1941).

ELIZABETH STUART PHELPS WARD (1844-1911), baptized Mary Gray, was born in Boston, the daughter of an Andover Theology Seminary professor and a writer. She was strongly influenced by her mother, who apparently chafed at her role as mere minister's wife, and whose writing contained feminist thought as well as the religious sentiment that made it popular. The original Elizabeth Stuart Phelps died when Mary Gray was eight, and the child then took her mother's name. The boy whom Phelps loved was killed in the Civil War. Phelps (later Ward) was an active supporter of women's rights, an antivivisectionist, and a prolific writer. Her most famous novel, *The Gates Ajar* (1868), was part of a trilogy; together with *Beyond the Gates* (1883) and *The Gates Between* (1887) it laid out her program for societal avenues to women's fulfillment. Interestingly, she is said to have suffered from "nervous disorders."

EUDORA WELTY (1909-   ) was born and lives in Jackson, Mississippi. She attended Mississippi State College for Women, received her B.A. from the University of Wisconsin, and attended graduate school at Columbia University. After working as a WPA photographer and writer, she began her luminous career in fiction. Her novels include *Delta Wedding* (1946), *Losing Battles* (1970), and *The Optimist's Daughter* (1972). Among her volumes of short stories are *A Curtain of Green* (1941), *The Wide Net* (1943), and *The Golden Apples* (1949)—though the complete collection is *The Collected Stories of Eudora Welty* (1980). She has won the highest honors and awards in the field of American letters, including the Gold Medal for the Novel conferred by the American Academy and Institute of Arts and Letters, the American Book Award, and the Pulitzer Prize.

CONSTANCE FENIMORE WOOLSON (1840-1894) was born in Claremont, New Hampshire, attended the Cleveland Young Ladies Seminary, and was graduated from Madame Chegary's School at New York. Surprisingly, her father, who had been considered a wealthy man, left no money when he died, and Woolson then supported herself by writing. From 1879 on she lived, traveled, and worked in Europe, producing many novels (including *Anne* [1882], *For the Major* [1883], and *Horace Chase* [1894]) and short stories. She died in Italy in a fall from her window; whether the incident was a suicide or an accident is still debated.